My Dad's Teenage Years by the Sea

THOMAS BIGGLEY

Published by Thomas Biggley

Published April 2021
Copyright © 2021 Thomas Biggley

Contents

Introduction

My name is Tommy. I have written a book of short stories about my life. I was born in Scotland. I ended up running away from my home. I found myself homeless by the sea in England. I lived with a drug addiction. I found Jesus Christ by the sea. Jesus Christ has transformed my life. I have shared that change in my short stories. I am not homeless today. I have been living in society for ten years. I hope you enjoy reading my short stories.

1

Adrift at sea like a piece of driftwood

I love to walk along a sandy beach. I like looking at all the driftwood on the beach. I picked a piece of driftwood up into my hands. The bit of driftwood was hollow inside. I am reminded that my soul was hollow. I spent my life trying to fill the gap in my soul. I filled the gap in my soul with drugs and crime. I was homeless by the sea. Jesus Christ took me as a hollow bit of driftwood. Jesus Christ filled the gap in my soul with the Holy Spirit. My life changed from that moment on.

I was no longer hollow on the inside. My piece of driftwood was ruff on the outside. This reminded me that I was a ruff teenager. I lived by the sea in my teenage years. I notice other people and they look content in life. They also have a hollowness in their souls. Some people have filled the gap in their souls with material wealth. We can fill the gap in our souls with the Holy Spirit. You will feel whole when the Holy Spirit dwells within you. I remember how empty I was.

Do you have that empty feeling inside your soul? Are you longing to fill that void in your soul? Jesus Christ came to fill us up and I am filled up. My love for you is pouring into a short story. Jesus Christ wants to know you in a personal way. Empty yourself of worldly things and let Jesus Christ in. I picked another piece of driftwood and it was smooth. Some people become smooth in their lives. I was smashed against the breakwater rocks in my young life. I was battered by my lifestyle.

A lot of people are beginning to realise that they feel lonely. I was lonely when I was homeless. Jesus Christ came into my life and I lost my loneliness. Have a look at what you are filling your life with. Does your material possession make you feel whole? A man can be rich, and he will say that he is empty. A man can be surrounded by family and friends and he will say that he is lonely. Jesus Christ can make you whole in your life. The Holy Spirit will fill you up with wisdom and spiritual riches.

My life has been shaped by the sea. I am writing a book of short stories for you. I want you to discover who Jesus Christ is. I know that Jesus Christ came to make us whole. So many people are feeling empty. The worlds riches do not fill the hollow gap in your soul. We are all bits of driftwood in the eyes of Jesus Christ. Some bits of driftwood are hollow. Other bits of driftwood are rotten. The list goes on. Invite Jesus Christ into your life if you are feeling hollow.

I know that Jesus Christ will make you feel whole. We are all going through similar things in our lives. We can ignore the empty feeling in our souls. We can cure that empty feeling by getting to know Jesus Christ. I was homeless in my teenage years. I never knew what it was like to live in a material world. I did not have a family when I was homeless. I just know that I was like a hollow bit of driftwood. I invited Jesus Christ into my life, and I changed my life. I have written a collection of short stories. I hope you find them interesting. You may end up feeling whole after you read them.

2

Watching families on the beach by the sea

I spent years homeless by the sea. I did not have a family. I was a runaway kid. No family wants you to be a part of their love and care when you are addicted to drugs. My family was all about drugs and crime. I had to run away from that life-style. I was not cut out for the destruction. I never ran away to find a family. I ran away to find myself. My mother was left heart broken when I ran away. Her only son disappeared without saying goodbye.

I was found and I was reunited with my mother for a day. We spent the day by the sea. I stayed by the sea and my mother returned home without her son. My mother died soon after she returned home. I watched families for years by the sea. Do families mean that much or do we take them for granted when we are by the sea. Running away from home takes courage. To stay a runaway breaks your heart. I do not cry anymore. I am a child of the creator of the mighty sea. Jesus Christ called the people who need of a family.

I did not have a family, so I ran into the arms of Jesus

Christ. The story of the prodigal son will show you a picture of how I found Jesus Christ. My birth father was addicted to drugs. My birth father loved me, but he could not help me escape the destruction of my drug addiction. I became a drug addict at a young age. I grew up in a criminal world. I ran away. I lived in my own little world. I lived with many regrets by the sea. Watching families building sandcastles did affect me.

What separated me from all the families on the beach. Was it my drug addiction or was it because I ran away from my family? Did I long to belong or did I think it was wrong to be that young runaway. Wright or wrong I knew that I would find my place in a dark world. I knew that running away was wrong but so was my old life at home. Violence brought me close to death. Everyone wanted to murder me in my old hometown. I now walk along a sandy beach. I know that I am not alone.

I smile because I found a love that families cannot buy. My love comes from the one who bore my sins upon the cross. I never envied families in my homeless years. I felt my loneliness in my homeless years. Jesus Christ set me apart from family's in my homeless years. I am happy to know that Jesus Christ loved me as he walked to the cross. I see so many broken families around me. I see the pain of the broken children in my deep sea. Jesus Christ can heal these broken families.

Jesus Christ could stop the children from becoming broken as teenagers. I was a broken teenager. I grew up in a broken family. I now sit by the sea. I can see that I do not need a family for Jesus Christ to love me. Are you living without a family in your life? Jesus Christ welcomes orphans into his family. I look at families on the beach. I want these families to know the love of Jesus Christ. A broken family can be restored in perfect grace. Jesus Christ should be the head of every family. Does your family need Jesus Christ at its centre?

3

Building a sandcastle on a sandy beach

A sandcastle is something everyone wants to build as they sit on a sandy beach. I watched people building sandcastles for years. I was alone by the sea, so I watched families building sandcastles. The sandcastles stood alone as the holiday makers made their way back to their hotels. I then watched the tide rolling in. The tide washed their sandcastles under its waves. I wanted to build something that the waves could not destroy. I could not build a life in my homelessness.

I was well damaged when I was homeless by the sea. I could build some foundations in the prison system. I had structure in the prison system. I am now a castle in the eyes of Jesus Christ. My castle is not built on a sandy beach. I isolated myself in my castle. I looked at your world. Your world did not want me to be a part of it. I had my defences when I was homeless. Everyone wanted to destroy my castle when I was homeless. I did not fear the streets when I was homeless.

I was sentenced to a drug treatment and testing order. One lady managed to penetrate the walls of my castle. My probation officer seen my lifestyle. She wanted to hear my story. I was on an order from the courts, so I had to comply with the probation team. This probation officer asked me why I was living on the streets. I told her and we started to work on my drug addiction. This probation officer became my mentor. This probation officer set me onto a new path.

Jesus Christ then came knocking on the door of my castle. Jesus Christ changed my life. You have a foundation when you accept Jesus Christ into your life. You can build your foundations on the teachings of Jesus Christ. The waves of the sea cannot wash your castle away. The castles of foolish men have been breached by the enemy. The walls of their castles have been torn down by the enemy. Let us have a look at Jesus Christ as a castle. Satan tried to penetrate the walls of God's castle for forty days and nights.

Jesus Christ calls us to build our lives on his teachings. I am a castle. I have built my life on the teachings of Jesus Christ. My walls are high. The arrows of Satan cannot reach me. Satan cannot shake my foundations because they are built on the teachings of Jesus Christ. Anyone can build a sandcastle on a sandy beach. I watched the waves of the sea and it washed the sandcastles under its waves. My old castle was week when I was homeless.

Satan destroyed my castle in my drug addiction. Jesus Christ came into my life. I started rebuilding my walls on his teachings. I am now a fortress against the darkness. My castle is now full of light. I invited the Holy Spirit into my life. The Holy Spirit changed my life. How does Jesus Christ see you as a castle? Build your foundations on his teachings today. Jesus Christ is calling you to be a castle. Satan wants to tear down your walls. You must protect yourself from the darkness. My castle is now a fortress. I feel secure in my castle. Jesus Christ is protecting me from the darkness.

4

Drawn to the sea in prayer

I lived by the sea for years. It was me and the mighty sea. I was not drawn to the sea in my teenage years. I sat by the sea. I put my back to your world. I now realise that I am drawn back to the sea. What draws me back to the sea with a pen and paper. I now sit by the sea. I can see that I am no longer a slave. Jesus Christ rescued me just in time. No one wanted to walk on a sandy beach with me in my homeless years. No one threw me a lifeline when I was homeless.

I love to write about the sea. Jesus Christ taught by the sea of galilee. Imagine Jesus Christ calling some fishermen by the sea. I can picture the crowds standing around Jesus Christ. These people were drawn to the sea. Fishermen were drawn from their fishing boats. I am drawn to the sea for many reasons. I received many gifts as a sat by the sea. I asked Jesus Christ to give me his gifts. The Holy Spirit looks for humble people like me. The waves of living waters washed my past away. I do miss the freedom of my homeless years.

I now have a home away from the sea. To many people do not contemplate their lives by the sea. To know that Jesus Christ taught by the sea is a blessing for me. I wish people would open their blind eyes to Jesus Christ. There is a force that draws people away from the sea. People are living in a concrete world. Jesus Christ is calling us to sit by the sea. I know that Jesus Christ draws people in when they are sitting by the sea. I am always sitting by the sea. I look out over the waves.

I can see that I am not alone. I am drawn in to watch a beautiful sunset. Would you drop your pride and search for Jesus Christ by the sea? Draw close to Jesus Christ and he will draw close to you. I will sit here. I will watch the waves of the sea. Jesus Christ is pulling the waves back. The sandy beach will be perfectly laid out before my eyes. I will be drawn to walk out with the tide. I will look back towards your concrete world. I am then remined that the world wants to draw me in.

I will not be drawn into a world of sin. I am free when I sit by the sea. Does your concrete world draw you in. The concrete world is full of bitterness and envy. I missed all that bitterness when I was homeless by the sea. I used to plant my eyes on the waves of the sea. I now plant my eyes on Jesus Christ. Find yourself a sandy beach. Let Jesus Christ draw you in. You need to be drawn away from your concrete world. You will be set free when you find Jesus Christ by the sea.

I am sitting by the sea today. I will be drawn back home. I will have to walk through the concrete streets. I am ok because I will be drawn back to the sea on another day. I just want the world to know that Jesus Christ pulled me away from a life of homelessness and drug addiction. Would you let Jesus Christ pull you away from a life of sin? You will be drawn into a relationship with Jesus Christ when you ditch your sins. Do not let your sins draw you away from Jesus Christ. Let Jesus Christ draw you towards the old, rugged cross.

5

Jesus Christ is our lighthouse by the sea

A lighthouse is more than a house to me. Jesus Christ was sent into a dark world by his father. Jesus Christ was to become a lighthouse to your dark world. How can I recognize the people who are stuck in darkness if I did not have a light in my life? People who do not accept Jesus Christ as light are stuck in darkness. I lay in a prison cell for twenty-three hours a day. The bright sun in exercise yard was far too bright for my hazy eyes. I relate my life to the sea.

There are thousands of lighthouses around the coast. The lighthouses are to bring the ships into a harbour. Jesus Christ is calling everyone who wants to find a harbour. My life started in darkness. The darkness had claimed my streets. Jesus Christ can draw people into his father's light. People are stuck in depression. I know that Jesus Christ could be their light. The darkness has old people trapped at home in isolation. The darkness has young people trapped in drug addiction.

The darkness has some people believing that they are worthless in this world. I help the old people who are trapped in isolation. I help the young people who are trapped in drug addiction. I give gifts to the people who feel worthless. I have showed you three things in the darkness. I have showed you the three good things that I do to beat the darkness. I am not winning the fight against the darkness. This is where my lighthouse comes into play.

The light of the world is my defence against the darkness. The Holy Spirit lights up my path. I am a beacon of hope to the people who are trapped in darkness. I take my light into the darkness. I march into the darkness. I declare that Jesus Christ is my light. I must fight a good fight to keep my light shining. My ink just flows when I shelter in the light of Jesus Christ. I am just a house to you. My body is a house in the eyes of Jesus Christ. I read the teachings of Jesus Christ and they light up my soul. The fight can take its toll on my life.

I keep the lights on in my own ways. Sitting by the sea with a pen and paper makes me feel bright. I will just be a house if I cover myself in sin. I will dampen down the light if I take the drugs. I am not just a house by the sea. I am a little light-house in the eyes of Jesus Christ. I had to be homeless by the sea in my teenage years. I learned about lighthouses when I was homeless. I was looking for a light in my dark nights.

I am blessed to say that I found Jesus Christ when I was living in the darkness. Are you looking for light in your own darkness? Call on Jesus Christ. Tell Jesus Christ that you are a sinner. The light of the world came to save you from the darkness of sin. Read the teachings of Jesus Christ and you will start to shine like a lighthouse. The Holy Bible is full of light. Do you believe that Jesus Christ is the light of the world? I had to be living in darkness to see that Jesus Christ is my light. Jesus Christ could be your light. Are you are living in darkness? Do not spent your life stumbling in the darkness of sin.

6

Holding a grain of sand in my hand

I love sand for many reasons. I like to sit and think on a sandy beach. My favourite sand is when it is blowing in the wind. I call it drifting sand. Where was my life blowing me when I was growing up as a kid? I was not like everyone else. Other people got blown along with the wind. I was like wet sand when I was growing up. I never got blown anywhere. No schooling or college. No university or a career. I never got the opportunities. I was brought up around drug addiction.

I was born and raised in darkness. I now sit on a sandy beach with a handful of sand. I watch as the sand trickles through my fingers. Each grain of sand represents a missed opportunity. I found one grain of sand in my life. I lost thousands of opportunities. I was left with one grain of sand. That one grain of sand is Jesus Christ. Some people got the thousand opportunities in life. They missed the greatest one ever given to this world. I have now become a dry grain of sand.

The Holy Spirit blows my thoughts onto my paper. I think of sand. I relate it to my life. Satan wants to snatch my grain of sand out of my hand. Satan tempts me with sin and selfish pleasures. I tell Satan to keep his thousand selfish pleasures. I tell Satan that I have my one grain of sand. My grain of sand satisfies my thirsty soul. My grain of sand brings me happiness by the sea. Satan tries to set a trap for me. I am smart because I lived by the sea. Satan sets out his quicksand for me.

Satan thinks that I will walk into his quicksand. It is nice walking on a sandy beach of selfish pleasures. It is nice until you find yourself in the sinking sand. I was not worth looking at when I was homeless. I knew it and I felt the shame of my past. I now have a grain of sand in my hand. I see Jesus Christ as a grain of sand. Would you give up a thousand selfish pleasures to hold Jesus Christ as your grain of sand. I watched my hand full of sand as it trinkled through my fingers.

I was left with one grain of sand in my hand. That grain

of sand turned out to be Jesus Christ. I tell people that Jesus Christ is like a grain of sand. I also tell them that they have a handful of sand. People do not like it when you tell them to give up a thousand selfish pleasures. You must give up a thousand selfish pleasures if you want to find the special grain of sand. No one can steel my special grain of sand. I spent years looking for it. A life of homelessness made it easy for me.

Your world offers me a thousand grains of selfish pleasures. I tell your world to keep its thousand grains of selfish pleasures. Search your life. Do you need to find this special grain of sand? This special grain of sand will satisfy your thirsty soul. This special grain of sand will bring you happiness and joy by the sea. Jesus Christ is like a special grain of sand. You can search the Holy Bible for this special grain of sand. You will become special in the eyes of Jesus Christ when you give up your selfish sins. You can repent for a thousand sins. Jesus Christ will then set you apart if you believe.

7

Listening to the waves of the sea

I spent a lot of time by the sea. I was looking out at the waves of the sea. I wanted the waves of the sea to speak to me. The waves of the sea told me that I was lost. I asked the waves of the sea to wash me back home. I knew that the waves could not wash me back home. I am pleased to say that Jesus Christ washed over me. A tide of love swept over me as I spoke to the waves of the sea. Other people are being washed in waves of guilt and shame.

People do not know that Satan is like a freak wave. I sit by the sea. I listen to the waves of the sea. Jesus Christ spoke to the waves in a storm. We are to listen to the voice of Jesus Christ. I struggle to hear the voice of Jesus Christ when I am trapped in your concrete world. I can hear the voice of Jesus Christ when I sit at the waves of the sea. People flocked to the sea when Jesus Christ taught by the sea of galilee. I know people who live in a noisy world. We are called to listen for the voice of Jesus Christ.

I am sitting at the waves of the sea today. I cannot hear the noise of the world. The gentle waves are lapping at my feet. I read a passage of my Holy Bible. It soaks into my soul. I will go back into your world. My ears will hear a lot of rubbish. I walk on the concrete streets. The traffic is loud. I walk through the shopping centre. The gossip is plain to hear. I go into a house and the t v is blaring out noise. I cannot hear Jesus Christ in a noisy world. I need to escape to a sandy beach.

Watching a sunset by the sea is amazing grace. You can catch a glimpse of Jesus Christ in a sunset. I watch other people as they walk along on a sandy beach. Their eyes are focused on a mobile phone. One or two people will take a photo of the sunset. These people just walk away with their eyes fixed on their phones. They do not sit and listen to the waves of the sea. It is too difficult to listen for the voice of

Jesus Christ by the sea. I was homeless by the sea. I learned to listen to the waves.

I never had a home with a tv. My eyes were fixed on the waves of the sea. I woke up as the sun was rising. I sat at the waves of the sea. I spoke with God. I then found Jesus Christ and he started to speak to me. I sat at the waves of the sea with my Holy Bible. The Holy Bible is a living book. You will hear the voice of Jesus Christ if you read your Holy Bible in front of the sea. I read a passage and I let it whirl around my head. The waves lap at my feet and I start to rest in God's amazing grace.

The Holy Bible has a voice of its own. I love to read about the sea of galilee. I then sit by the waves of the sea. My mind starts to take a picture of that time. I can picture Jesus Christ calling for a fisherman's boat. Jesus Christ taught from a fisherman's boat. The people were standing at the waves of the sea. These people heard the voice of Jesus Christ as the waves where lapping at their feet. We can listen to that same Jesus Christ today. We have his teachings in the Holy Bible. I listened to the waves of the sea. This is the short story that I came up with for you.

8

Traveling around the coastline of the sea

It is my dream to travel around the coastline of Britain. I will travel around the coastline in a little camper van. It will be me and my dog. I am hoping to take a wife. I will have to find a wife who will delight in my love for Jesus Christ. I was once coasting through my life as a homeless teenager. I was washed in waves of my own blood. I grew up and it was ok to drink and take drugs. I grew up around it all. I got addicted to heroin. I was no longer coasting's through my life.

I had to runaway to the seaside. I was living by the sea and I was not coasting. My life beat me, and it nearly cost me my life. I did not find a lovely wife by the sea. My drug addiction would not let me travel around the coast. I was anchored to one part of the seaside. I had a three mile stretch of coastline to myself. I often found myself doing a prison sentence. I used to dream about travelling around the coastline of Britain. I was cast out of prison on a fishing line. I landed back on my three miles of coastline.

Would I ever get reeled in from my stretch of coastline? Yes, is the answer to that question. Jesus Christ is the one who reeled me in from my coastline. I was like a wild fish when Jesus Christ started to reel me in from my coastline. I fought hard to escape back into my world of homelessness. I was not cut out for living in your society. Your society looked at me with disgust when I was homeless on the streets. Your society cast me out and I can now reel them in.

I will travel the coast of Britain with Jesus Christ as my guide. I will tell people how Jesus Christ set me free by the sea. I now live in a home with my little dog. I always come back to the sea with my pen and paper. I can now cast out my short stories about my time by the sea. Three words changed my life. I left the seaside for three words of truth. Fisher of men is the words that changed my life. Jesus Christ said follow me and I will make you a fisher of men. I was not a man when Jesus Christ reeled me in from the coastline.

I was a broken teenager. I had just left my twenty's. I was touching thirty years old. I am now forty years old. I am planning a trip of a lifetime. How free will I be when I set of in my little camper van. I am still as poor as I was when I was homeless. I will sell my book in the thousands. That will fund my trip. I can share my testimony with other people. The last ten years has been amazing grace. I have severed Jesus Christ as a fisher of men. I have hooked a lot of broken souls for Jesus Christ. I will have to share my life story in a book. I always come back to this stretch of coastline.

It is special for me to sit here for a while. This will be my starting place for the trip of a lifetime. Would you let Jesus Christ call you on a journey of a lifetime? We are called to travel with the good news. Your coastline could be your career or anything that holds you back from following Jesus

Christ. let Jesus Christ real you in and he will change your life. I will be documenting my trip of a lifetime. Look out for a new book about me travelling around the coastline.

9

Shipwrecked in a stormy sea

I love to walk along a sandy beach. I like to look at the remains of the shipwrecks. The shipwrecks are popping out of the sand. These are the ships that once sailed over the mighty sea. I wish the remains could tell me a story. I want to know about the storm that shipwrecked these ships. These mighty ships sailed over the waves with my confidence. I ponder about my own young life. I never started out as a mighty ship. I did become a shipwreck. I was born to be shipwrecked in my young life.

I was shipwrecked in homelessness. I think that I was lucky. I feel for the people who were once beautiful ships. I young promising footballer was shipwrecked in drug addiction. A solider in the army had the prospect of rising the ranks and he was shipwrecked in drug addiction. It is such a shame. It is too painful for me to list the people who were shipwrecked in drug addiction. These people are now lost in your dark world. Some of them are living in homelessness. Others are rotting away in a prison cell.

I do not need to wonder about my life. I was always going

to be a tragic shipwreck. My birth father was addicted to drugs. A son should never inject drugs with his birth father. I regret that moment in my life. My father was also a shipwreck. I look at the shipwrecks that are popping out of the sandy beach. I have nothing to boast about in my life. I will boast about the glory of Jesus Christ. My Jesus Christ took me as a shipwreck. Jesus Christ started to rebuild me into a mighty ship.

Jesus Christ can also rebuild the shipwrecks that are homeless. It may be too late for them to be a footballer or a sergeant in the army. Jesus Christ can make them greater than all of them things. I am a new ship. I am protected by grace. I sail through my life for Jesus Christ. Some people want to see me as a shipwreck again. Jesus Christ will not let me run aground. A storm looks to topple my ship and I call out to my Lord. The disciples where in a storm with Jesus Christ.

The panic-stricken disciples called out to Jesus Christ. Jesus Christ said oh you of little faith. Jesus Christ raised his hands over the stormy sea. There was a stillness on the surface of the sea. I know that Jesus Christ does that in my life. I do run aground sometimes but that is what this life does to you. Jesus Christ now uses me to help the other shipwrecks. I tell them my story and they want to know more about Jesus Christ.

I have seen shipwrecks being restored in the name of Jesus Christ. Never pass a shipwreck and say that it cannot be sailed again. My Jesus Christ restored me. I have sailed the seven seas for Jesus Christ. I love to help other shipwrecks. I have seen them being restored in perfect grace. Do you feel like a shipwreck? Jesus Christ can restore you into a mighty ship. Look at my story with Jesus Christ. I was the worst shipwreck known to man. I am now sharing my story for the shipwrecks. The Holy Bible has the power to restore your broken soul. I pray that you will become a mighty ship for Jesus Christ.

10

Jesus Christ is my anchor in a storm

I love to look at the anchor on a ship. I know that it is to anchor a ship in a storm. My teenage years where like a ship. I did not have an anchor to hold me in the storms of life. I was adrift at sea in my homelessness. A ship without an anchor is just a dangerous vessel. I was not a dangerous person in my young life. I was like a ship. Everyone bailed out on me. I was left to sail through my teenage years on my own. I do not look for glory by saying that I became a captain.

I was looking for an anchor for my soul. I battled through my stormy sea on my own. I was hungry and homeless in my drug addiction. I became isolated in a stormy sea. Some people said that I was a lost cause in a stormy sea. The people who abandoned me are starting to wish they were like me.

I now have heavens anchor on my ship. Jesus Christ is the anchor that holds me in the storms of life. Jesus Christ was an anchor to his disciples. Jesus Christ came into my sinking ship.

Jesus Christ said do not fear my child. The Lord Jesus Christ is near to the people who are afraid. I was fearful when Jesus Christ anchored my ship. I was a runaway on the streets. Jesus Christ wanted to anchor me in your society. I spent my life a drift at sea. I now anchor my ship to Jesus Christ. I see the people who bailed out on me. The people in your society left me adrift in my homelessness. I tell these people that I have found an anchor for my ship.

They looked puzzled at me in my physical poverty. They tell me that I am living on a raft of poverty. I was living on a raft of poverty and these people were living on luxury ships. I insist on telling them about my anchor. They mock me because they have material wealth as their anchor. I can tell you that I love my raft of physical poverty. Jesus Christ came to anchor the humble sinners. I have shared my anchor with humble people. I took the poor people to my local church. The poor people are now anchored down to Jesus Christ.

The storms will rage over this sinful land. The rich fools will be shipwrecked in selfish pride. What are you anchored to in your sinful life? Is it your material wealth or maybe it is your family? I had none of these things when I was homeless, so I accepted Jesus Christ as my anchor. Life will toss me in all directions, and I smile. I smile because I am anchored to the teachings of Jesus Christ. I know people who are being tossed around in a storm. Their sinful lives are turning them into a shipwreck.

They mock me when I tell them about my anchor. I am anchored down with my pen and paper. I sit by the sea. I know that my soul is anchored to Jesus Christ. My soul is my ship. Jesus Christ is my anchor. Your flesh is probably anchored down to a material world. You know that your soul is being tossed around in a sea of fear. Call out to Jesus Christ. Ask Jesus Christ to anchor your soul to his father's grace. You will be held in perfect peace when you bow down at the foot of the old, rugged cross. Let Jesus Christ anchor you to his amazing grace. I am anchored to God's amazing grace in my life.

11

Jesus Christ is the captain of my ship

I think of the responsibility that a captain has when he is sitting at the wheel of his mighty ship. How does the captain feel when his crew puts their trust in him? Look back to before a ship got a navigation system built into it. The captain was trusted to navigate the stormy sea. I think about the Apostle Paul in the Holy Bible. The Apostle Paul was in a few disasters at sea. The Apostle Paul advised the captain about a trip. The captain ignored the Apostle Paul.

They ended up shipwrecked. Jesus Christ said do not boast

but the Apostle Paul had stuff to boast about. I could go on and write a short book about the Apostle Paul. Jesus Christ was the captain of the Apostle Pauls ship. I want to be like the Apostle Paul. I said lord Jesus Christ you are the captain of my ship. Some people are not willing to let Jesus Christ captain their ships. We are called to hand over the captain's wheel to Jesus Christ. I look at my life when I try to captain my own ship.

I sail into the storms when Jesus Christ gives me the captains wheel. I am not ashamed to say that I need Jesus Christ to be my captain. Life can get stormy at times in my life. I can relax because Jesus Christ is my captain. Some people appear to be sailing in a calm sea. I got to know these people and they are sailing in the storms. Some people are prepared to let Jesus Christ captain their ships on a Sunday morning. They take the captains wheel back on a Monday morning.

These people are not letting Jesus Christ be their captain. The things of this world are sailing their ships into the rocks. What would Jesus Christ do with their captains' wheel in the week. Jesus Christ would probably sail them into a midweek bible study. Jesus Christ will talk them into helping the homeless. Jesus Christ would not sail them into the rocks. I have let Jesus Christ captain my ship for the last ten years. It has been stormy at times. It has been calm at times.

The most important thing is my Jesus Christ is to be trusted. Look at the Apostle Paul when he gave Jesus Christ the captains wheel. I am a passenger on my ship because Jesus Christ is my captain. Would you hand over your captain's wheel to Jesus Christ. It takes faith to put your trust in Jesus Christ. I had no direction in my homeless years. I did not have a captain on my ship. I now sail through my life with Jesus Christ at the captain's wheel. Give Jesus Christ your captains wheel.

Let Jesus Christ sail you through this life. My life is exciting. I have a destination to my life. I tried to be the captain of my ship and I got lost. I put my hands up. I told Jesus Christ to take the captain's wheel. Would you raise your hands away from your captains' wheel and put your trust in Jesus Christ? Jesus Christ was sent to guide us through this stormy life. Are you feeling lost in a sea of worries? You do not have to worry when Jesus Christ captains your ship. I let Jesus Christ have the captain's wheel of my ship. I have sailed in amazing grace for the last ten years with Jesus Christ.

12
Resting on a bench by the sea

I spent a lot of time resting on benches by the sea. My twenties were spent in homelessness. The sea was special to me in my teenage years. I sat looking out over the waves. Watching the tides unravelled my life. My thoughts where clear to hear. Why did I spent so much time resting by the sea? Your world beat me up, so I rested myself by the sea. I was also on the run from the authorities. A lot of people wanted to murder me as well. My drug addiction did not want me to rest.

I looked to your world with my back facing the sea. My whole life was lived on the edge of danger. My body was ravaged by my lifestyle. I slept on the benches in the summer months. I am now resting on a bench in my recovery. Jesus Christ calls us to rest in his presence. Jesus Christ is willing to rest your tormented soul. I found the rest that I needed in my young life. I found rest from within myself. The guilt and shame were not mine, so I gave them to Jesus Christ.

Your guilt and shame will never let you rest in the presence of Jesus Christ. Why do so many people refuse to believe that Jesus Christ can give them rest. I look at people in the real world. These people are restless. I met a man. This man was restless in his soul. I prayed for him and the weight on his shoulders left him. I took him along to a church. This man started to find his rest. This man's soul got lighter and lighter. I know that the Holy Spirit was at work in his life.

I put the groundwork in to keep my soul light. This man would not do the things that I suggested. The weight returned to his shoulders. The man became bitter again. It is so sad because I put time and energy into helping this man. I have helped people to find their rest in Jesus Christ. Some people are happy, and they follow Jesus Christ to the cross. Other people are too lazy to follow Jesus Christ. I follow Jesus Christ and I rest in his presence. I sit on my bench and I wonder why Jesus Christ loved me.

I know people and they are terribly busy in their lives. The world keeps them busy. Their sinful flesh is always lusting after material things. The material things of this world will leave you restless. Jesus Christ called out to the wary. Jesus Christ said come unto me and I will give you rest. I had to be homeless for Jesus Christ to call me. I used to lie in a prison cell, and I was restless. I was homeless and I was always nervous. I found Jesus Christ and my mind is now at peace.

There are no worries in my life. Your world can survive without me. I asked someone to take ten minutes out their day to read the Holy Bible. They asked me if I was crazy or mad. I am crazy because I could read my Holy Bible for ten hours a day. The Holy Bible gives you the rest that you need. The teachings of Jesus Christ will give rest to your tormented soul. You will rest in perfect grace when you put the teaching of Jesus Christ into practice. Jesus Christ is calling out to the restless. Are you feeling restless in your mind? Find a bench by the sea and pray. You will meet Jesus Christ in your restfulness.

13
Watching fishermen by the sea

I am sitting by the sea today. I can see about twelve fishermen. They are standing and sitting at the waves of the sea. I now think about what I am fishing for in my own life. I do this most days of the week. The fishermen are looking at the tips of their fishing rods. I could ask the fishermen what they are fishing for in their personal life's. The fishermen would be shocked because they get asked if they have caught any fish. My mind wonders to Jesus Christ walking along the sea of galilee.

Jesus Christ called a few fishermen from their boats. Jesus Christ told the fisher men that he would make them a fisher of men. Could Jesus Christ call these men away from their fishing rods. I am watching these men and they look humble. The disciples left their fishing boats to follow Jesus Christ to the cross. One man is reeling his fishing line in. It is just a change of bait. The man has not caught a fish. I am doing a bit of fishing from my car. I do not have a physical fishing rod.

I just cast out my tears and fears. I tell Jesus Christ that there is a weight on the end of my line. The weight is the fears I have about living in the real world. I used to be free in my homeless years. A fisher man is putting some bait on his hook. The fisherman is hoping to lure a prize fish. I watch as he cast out his fishing line. Do the men know that they could cast out their fears to Jesus Christ? Do the fishermen know that they can reel the promises of Jesus Christ in?

The fishermen love to fish by the sea. These men are escaping their real problems in the real world. One fisherman could be escaping from his broken marriage. Another fisherman could be hiding away from his fears. The tide will draw out. The fishermen will return to the real world. There is also a line of cars. They are looking out over the fishermen. There is an old couple with a flask of tea and a newspaper. Some people are on their own. Are they looking for the meaning to their lives?

There are a couple of young ladies in a car next to mine. They are chatting away about their lives. Jesus Christ told his disciples to cast their nets to the right. I would have to be mad to do the same with these fishermen. I leave my thoughts with Jesus Christ by a fire. WitchWhich disciple jumped out of the boat to meet Jesus Christ on the shoreline. My thoughts bring tears to my eyes. I used to be so free by this sea. I now must live in the real world. Jesus Christ calls us to be a fisher of men.

I pause to pray for the fishermen. I also pray for the old couple with a flask of tea. One of them has fallen asleep. The other one is reading a newspaper. I am being distracted by the pretty girls in the car next to mine. I am now going into your concrete world. Would you love to become a fisher of men for Jesus Christ? The disciples of Jesus Christ became a fisher of men. Thousands of people were caught at Pentecost. I have caught a lot of lost souls for Jesus Christ. I reeled them into church. I then watched them changing their lives for Jesus Christ.

14
Finding rubbish on a sandy beach

I do not like to see rubbish on my sandy beach. I sit on my bench. I look at what the tide has drawn in. I spot the rubbish amongst the seaweed. A team of beach cleaners are making their way down the beach. They have litter sticks and bags in their hands. They are picking the rubbish out of the seaweed. I love to walk along a clean beach. I am thankful to these men and women. I will come back here tomorrow. There will be more rubbish amongst the seaweed.

The litter is being washed in at night. I know that Satan is like the tide at night. Satan washes rubbish in on my personal life. My personal rubbish is my fears and worries. Satan is crafty in his attempts to draw me away from following Jesus Christ. I fight harder in my prayers. I asked Jesus Christ to stop the worries and fears. You could spend a lifetime picking rubbish from the sandy beach. It is not pointless for the litter pickers to do their jobs. I must rid myself of my tears and fears. I read the Holy Bible as much as I can.

My life is utterly rubbish if I forget the teachings of Jesus Christ. I fight the good fight to keep my head clear of my fears and worries. I can now walk along a perfect beach. The litter pickers have done a great job. I know some people and they are fools. These people love to collect spiritual rubbish. You can see that their lives are messy. Can these people help it or are they hoarders? We read about hoarders with material rubbish. They fill their homes with rubbish.

It is the same with spiritual rubbish. People overload their lives with mental and spiritual rubbish. People love to collect gossip from their friends. These people then spread the lies and deceit around a rubbish tip. Society is a rubbish tip to me. Your society is full of negative rubbish. I was free from society's rubbish tip when I was homeless by the sea. The waves of the sea will not tell you negative stuff. A sunset over the sea speaks of God's creation. Jesus Christ has put me in your society.

I fought hard to be free by the sea. People love to tell me their gossip and lies. One person will say did you hear what happened with so and so. I stop them. I tell them that I do not want to hear it. It is always a bad news story. I do not like to hear bad news. I ask Jesus Christ why he brought me away from the sea. Jesus Christ said my child I want you to warn people about spiritual rubbish. I am telling you to beware of spiritual rubbish.

Tell people that they are hoarders of material rubbish and they will deny it. Tell people that they are hoarders of spiritual rubbish and they will not like it. I am not happy about living in society's rubbish tip, but I do it for Jesus Christ. I have been fighting against the spiritual rubbish for ten years. I must sit by the sea. I must pick through all the gossip of lies. My head is now clear, and I can hear the waves of the sea. I am not a rubbish writer. My ink does not collet your spiritual rubbish. Now stop littering my beach with your material rubbish.

15

Oars on a rowing boat in a storm

I went on a rowing boat with two oars. I now realise how difficult it is to row over the water. I lost one oar in the water. I now relate rowing to my personal life. I was left with one oar. I was going around in a circle. That is all you can do when you have one oar. I had no oars in my homeless years. I was stuck in the middle of the water without my oars. I have good news today. I now have two oars on my rowing boat. I now row through my life with Jesus Christ.

I can sail through my life if I work my oars for Jesus Christ. Imagine yourself as rowing boat in my short story. Life can get difficult when you are rowing against a tide of fear. I can row over the waves of my fears because Jesus Christ is in my rowing boat. My spirit is so strong today. I sit by the sea. I see myself as a rowing boat. Jesus Christ gave me a pair of oars. I have used my oars. I was a homeless teenager. I am now a grown man. The last ten years have been tough. I look back on my life. I can see how far I have travelled.

I tried to row away from Jesus Christ in my teenage years. Jesus Christ was taking me in one direction. I was trying to row back into my old lifestyle. Try and sit in a rowing boat with someone. Imagine you have one oar each. Try and go in a straight line. You will see that it is impossible. It is like that with me and Jesus Christ. My flesh wants me to row me back into a stormy sea. Jesus Christ wants to row me into a sea living waters.

I did not think that deserved to sail in a calm sea with Jesus Christ. I now realise that Jesus Christ has used my past. I have shown people how to row towards Jesus Christ. Some of them gave up and that is a shame. One or two of them took my advice and that makes me happy. Some people row for Jesus Christ on a Sunday. They then row away from

Jesus Christ on a Monday. I never got to this stage by my own strength. The teachings of Jesus Christ kept me rowing towards the cross. It takes great faith to believe in my story.

I was a homeless teenager. My old rowing boat had holes in it. Are you feeling like an old rowing boat? Are your personal problems sinking your rowing boat into the sea? Look to Jesus Christ if you are like I was in my old life. Put your hands up and give Jesus Christ the oars to your rowing boat. Jesus Christ will lead you in a new direction. The new direction will be difficult because you are a selfish person. You have rowed through this life for the things of this world.

The things of this world will leave you going around in circles. Do not let Satan control the direction that you are going in. Invite Jesus Christ into your selfish rowing boat. Never give up because Jesus Christ is calling you to row towards the cross. Are you prepared to row away from your selfish sins? This world will have you rowing for success. That success will rob you of life. I now row through my life with Jesus Christ. I sometimes put my oars away. I put my sails up and Jesus Christ blows a holy wing through my soul.

16

Looking at the surface of the sea

I used to watch the different colours on the surface of the sea. Bits of the ocean's surface were dark and other bits where lighter. My old life was lived in the darker parts of the ocean's surface. I never experienced the lighter parts of the ocean's surface. I was born into the darker parts of the ocean's surface. I looked at people from my homelessness. They seemed to be living in the lighter parts of the ocean's surface.

I was just a homeless teenager who longed to experience a different way of life. Only the foolish would swim with me in teenage years. Jesus Christ came into my life. Jesus Christ dragged me into the lighter parts of the ocean's surface. Why would Jesus Christ pull me out of my dark sea of spiritual poverty. I would have drowned in a dark sea of spiritual poverty. Your world left me to drown in a dark sea of spiritual poverty. Jesus Christ rose from the grave to save me from my dark sea of spiritual poverty. Things got lighter in my dark sea of spiritual poverty.

What part of the sea are you living in today? Your friends will tell you that you are swimming in the lighter parts of the ocean's surface. You know that your selfish sins are holding you in the darker parts of the ocean's surface. A homeless person knows that he is swimming in the darker parts of the ocean's surface. I was that homeless person in my teenage years. I now swim in the lighter parts of the ocean's surface. Jesus Christ is calling you into a clear sea of living waters.

Do not be afraid to admit that you are drowning in the darker parts of the ocean's surface. We should not judge the people who are drowning in the darker parts of the ocean's surface. I can write about this subject because I lived by the sea in spiritual poverty. I watched the ocean's surface. The sun would split the clouds. A ray of sunshine would light up parts of the ocean's surface. I fought hard to stay in the darker parts of the ocean's surface. I now look at people in your society.

They appear to be swimming in the lighter parts of the ocean's surface. I got to know the people who judged me when I was a homeless teenager. There outward appearance told me that they were swimming in the lighter parts of the ocean's surface. I love the people who are swimming in the darker parts of the ocean's surface. They are open to hear about Jesus Christ. I show them that they are sinners in the eyes of Jesus Christ.

Do you know that your sins are holding you a prisoner in the darker parts of the ocean's surface? I found this subject difficult to write. I had to look at my past. My past can take its toll on my mental health. I now realise that my drug addiction kept me in the darker parts of the ocean's surface. Drag yourself away from your sins and you will bask in a sea of living waters. Do not spend your life in the darker parts of the ocean's surface. It is easier to stay in the darker parts of the ocean's surface. Jesus Christ is calling you towards the lighter parts of the ocean's surface.

17

Diving into a spiritual sea

I ended up living in a hostel. I got sentenced to a drug treatment testing order from the courts. I started to go to the swimming baths. I loved diving into the swimming pool. I would swim under the water while holding my breath. Popping out of the water breathless was a feeling of adrenaline. I thought that I could wash my guilt and shame away in a pool of chlorine. Drug addiction leaves you feeling shameful and guilty. Running away from home leaves you broken.

I did swim in the real sea. It was a red-hot summers day. I was swimming in the grip of my drug addiction. I felt free in the open sea. The swimming baths was cleaner than the open sea. I did not leave the swimming pool until my eyes stung. My hands and feet were shrivelled up by the chlorine. I stayed in the showers for a long time. Jumping from the hot shower into the cold shower was fun. I found Jesus Christ and he washed me clean in a sea of living waters. I was washed from within my soul.

I found myself in a church. This man said can I pray for you. I said yes. This man said can I lay my hands on you. I said yes. This man asked Jesus Christ to wash me clean. This man asked Jesus Christ to take my guilt and shame away. Jesus Christ did what a pool of chlorine could not do. This is a true story. I went on a journey of discovery with Jesus

Christ. I got myself dirty again. I ran away into my old life-style. I was not to be that clean in my life.

I got used to feeling guilty about running away from my home. The shame of homelessness and drug addiction belonged to me. This man asked Jesus Christ to wash me clean. Jesus Christ washed me a little to clean. My title about diving into the sea is for you. Jesus Christ has a sea of living waters. Dive in there if you are feeling guilty or ashamed. I have prayed for people to be washed clean. You can see that their eyes are sparkling clean. Their outward appearance looked dishevelled, but their soul was washed clean.

No one wants to admit that their souls are tainted in sin. Their outward appearance makes them whiter than snow. They love to judge the people who look dirty on the outside. I was judged in my homeless years. A man had the grace to ask Jesus Christ to wash me clean. I have accepted that I must stay clean. It took me years to finally admit that I needed to stay clean. I was dirtier than the physical sea. I lived a blooded life. I am not washing blood of my face today.

I am sharing my love for Jesus Christ. Do not judge a homeless person by his outward appearance. That homeless person's soul is just as dirty as his outward appearance. I love the homeless people. The homeless people know that their souls are tainted by sin. I live a cleaner way of life today. I will never forget how dirty my soul was. I do get myself dirty sometimes, but I have my Jesus Christ to was me clean. Do you feel that your life has left you feeling shameful and guilty? Are you feeling ashamed of your past sins? Ask Jesus Christ to wash you clean in a sea of living waters.

18

Looking into a rockpool by the sea

I stand and investigate a rockpool by the sea. What do I see in this rockpool? I can see my past and my reflection. I was born into a rockpool. My rockpool was a drug infested council estate. I grew up in a place of drugs and violence. This rockpool looks lifeless to my eyes. I lift a rock up and its teaming with life. Creatures are hiding in the rockpool. It is like that for some people in the drug infested council estates. People are hiding under rocks of depression and fear.

My old rockpool was full of child abuse and self-harm. It was a violent rockpool to me. I ran away from that rockpool. No one bends down to have a closer look at these rockpools of spiritual poverty. Kids are born into these rockpools of spiritual poverty and they become the rockpool. Each rockpool has a family that is known for the violence and crime. My family was really into the crime and violence. Most of my family were addicted to substances. The so-called gangsters sold their drugs to innocent kids.

The bullies and cowards exploit the poor people. The gangsters stand back as the kids are abused. They then feed the kids drugs to kill their pain. I could say a lot about the so-called gangsters. The pain goes deep with me. My story is nothing to be proud of. My drug infested council estate wanted me dead. I was left blooded and battered. I must admit that I caused my fair share of trouble. I robbed my way into the trouble. I climbed out of the rockpool before I was murdered.

I ran away into another rockpool. I was washed in my own blood again. I was a runaway in the eyes of the world. I found myself living by the sea. I have to say that Jesus Christ pulled me out of my rockpool. I escaped my rockpool. I then rested myself by the sea. Jesus Christ has a rockpool of living waters. There is no violence in a rockpool of living waters. I do not have to hide under a rock. My blood does not flow like it used to. I feel safe in a rockpool of living waters.

The last ten years has been amazing. Some people judge the rockpools of spiritual poverty. Jesus Christ has put me into my old rockpools. I went in to my old rockpools. I told the broken souls about my Jesus Christ. I cannot boast about it because I did it for Jesus Christ. I went into the rockpool where I grew up. What a story that is. I would have to write a book about it. I got the name of bible Tommy because I declared that Jesus Christ has a rockpool of living waters.

Do not judge the rockpools of spiritual poverty. Jesus Christ spent time in the rockpools of spiritual poverty. The Holy Bible tells us that Jesus Christ washed the unclean in amazing grace. Jesus Christ was born into a rockpool of problems. I know it is hard to believe but it is true. I know what rockpool I live in. I must admit that it was hard for me to leave my old rockpools. I got to visit them enough over the last ten years. Are you living in a rockpool of spiritual poverty? Pray to Jesus Christ and he will save you from your rockpool of spiritual poverty.

19

Surfing the waves of the sea with Jesus Christ

My life was not about surfing the mighty sea in my teenage years. I am sitting by the sea today. I am watching the kite surfers. What kind of life have they had in their young lives? These lads are surfing over the waves. I watch as the kites propels them over the waves. I know that their surfing boards are useless without the physical wind. I am now a kite surfer in my personal life. I surf through my personal life with Jesus Christ.

I do not need the earths wind to propel me through over my struggles. I pick up my Holy Bible. I read the inspired words of Jesus Christ. I have a holy wind blowing through my soul. The power of the Holy Spirit is with me in this short story. I know people who confess that they believe in Jesus Christ. They do not have a holy wind in their souls. A kite suffer finds the physical wind on a rare day. Part time believers find their holy wind on a rare Sunday. They are windless in the weekdays.

Believers could be sailing in amazing grace if they got their Holy Bibles out on a weekday. A surfer's kite and board are tucked away in his garage. A part time believers Holy Bible is tucked away in a cupboard. My suffering for Jesus Christ is done in the weekdays. In fact, I am surfing for twenty-four hours a day. I am sitting by the sea. I am crying out to the kite surfers. Do the kite surfers know that Jesus Christ has a spiritual wind in his hands? I know that their personal lives are windless.

I took a windless drug addict to church. I surfed myself around to his house this week. I gave him a Holy Bible. I then surfed through the gospels with him. It was a magic moment in my faith. I also surfed him around in my car. I was helping him to get into recovery. I put my time and energy into this young lad. I was doing a big talk in a church. I took him along. There was at least a hundred people. I just spoke to this lad. The holy wind in my soul spoke to him.

How is my life possible today? I watched kite suffers for years when I was homeless by the sea. I can now write about this subject because Jesus Christ blew my life apart. Sharing my faith is the key to surfing with Jesus Christ. The last ten years has been like that. I want the surfing boys to know Jesus Christ. I look at society and people are windless. They are looking for a quick fix. The posh surfing boys get an adrenalin kick out of surfing the mighty sea.

My life was totally different to their lives. Does your soul feel windless today? Are you driven through life by your greed for material wealth? Jesus Christ could propel you through your personal life. I am propelled to tell the world about my Jesus Christ. The disciples of Jesus Christ where windless in an upper room. Jesus Christ was no longer with them. A holy wind swept through the upper room. The disciples then sailed the good news about the risen Jesus Christ.

You can read about Pentecost in the Holy Bible. The disciples became suffers for Jesus Christ. I received a holy wind. Believe in Jesus Christ and you will receive a holy wind in your soul.

20

Jesus Christ threw me a life ring by the sea

I walk along the sea front. I notice some boxes. They have life rings in the boxes. The box has instructions on the front of it. Throw the life ring in the water if you see someone drowning. I was drowning on dryland. No one threw me a life ring. It was plain to see that I was homeless by the sea. No one took notice of me as I sat by the sea. People would run for a life ring if they saw someone drowning in the physical sea. People will save you if you are drowning in the physical sea.

You can forget about a rescue if you are drowning on dryland. I am not drowning on dryland today. I am saving the poor souls who are drowning on dryland. Jesus Christ threw me a spiritual life ring. My soul was drowning in a sea of guilt and shame. People on dryland will not admit that their souls are drowning in some sort of pain. People are too proud to cry out for a spiritual life ring. I was a homeless teenager. I was drowning in a sea of loneliness.

I now realise that normal people are drowning in loneliness. A person surround by family and friends can drown in a sea of loneliness. I am not lonely today. I have a friend in Jesus Christ. My spiritual life ring keeps my soul afloat. People never wanted to save me when I was drowning by the sea. Do you need a spiritual life ring for your soul? Your flesh will drown in the physical sea. Your soul will also drown in a spiritual sea. I look at the boxes with life rings in them.

Jesus Christ is speaking to me. Jesus Christ wants me to tell the world that heaven has boxes of spiritual life rings. They are not visible to your eyes. Imagine if we had spiritual boxes placed all over our streets. Imagine if they all held spiritual life rings. The instruction would be simple. The instructions would say call out to Jesus Christ. People on the brink of suicide could open the boxes. Their souls would be kept afloat. A family would not lose a loved one. I see a broken homeless person and I must open a spiritual box.

I tell them about my life, and they listen to me. I tell them that my soul was drowning in a sea of guilt and shame. We should be looking out for the drowning souls. A lot of people ignore the homeless because they are not drowning in the physical sea. This is turning out to be a nice story. Call out for a spiritual life ring if your soul is drowning in a sea of guilt and shame. We do not judge a person when we see them drowning in the sea. We just run for the physical life ring.

We do judge a person when we see them drowning on dryland. A homeless person looks like a drain on our taxes, so we do not throw them a spiritual life ring. I know what it is like to drown on dryland. I sat begging and people would not even look at me. I thought that they had it all together. Jesus Christ saved me, and I ended up living in your society. I got to know people is society. These people are drowning in a sea of problems. I know people who are drowning in a sea of depression. I tell them about my spiritual life ring. They want to receive the spiritual life ring. Do you need a spiritual life ring?

21

Being a fisherman for Jesus Christ

What did the disciples think when Jesus Christ called them from their boats? What meaning did they get from the words of a fisher of men. I found Jesus Christ. I understood what the words mean to me. I was caught. I then became a fisher of men. I love the disciples. The disciples left their fishing boats to follow Jesus Christ to the cross. Jesus Christ taught these humble men. The disciples received the Holy Spirit at Pentecost. The disciples then became a fisher of men.

Thousands of men were caught at Pentecost. The kingdom grew from Pentecost. The Holy Spirit enabled the disciples to travel far and wide. Satan tried to stop the disciples from catching men. Satan has a net. The net is the world. The world is full of material things. Sinful men are seeking material things. They are caught in the wrong net. The disciples left everything to become a fisher of men. I have become a fisher of men. I am always casting out my fishing rod. Jesus Christ is the bait on my hook.

I have seen people being reeled into a relationship with Jesus Christ. They were in a net of amazing grace. I also watched them being drawn back into the world. Jesus Christ is no longer in their lives. People are blind to the times. Jesus Christ will sweep a net for the final time. It is called the end times. A good fisherman lands his catch. The fisherman sorts the good fish from the bad fish. The good fisherman burns the bad fish because he does not want to catch them again.

I worry about the people who are not in a relationship with Jesus Christ. I work hard to bring people into a relationship with Jesus Christ. Will you be a good fish, or will you be a bad fish? The good fish will be separated from the bad fish. Us humans are fish in the eyes of Jesus Christ. I am fishing out this story as I contemplate my life by the sea. Let Jesus Christ reel you into a relationship with him. I look at the world. There are a lot of bad fish to be caught. I know that Jesus Christ hooked me with his amazing grace.

I was like a wild salmon in my teenage years. It took Jesus Christ a while to get me into his keep net. I fought to stay in my old lifestyle. The last ten years have taught me a lot. I love to see someone changing their lives for Jesus Christ. Are you afraid to be caught? You are a bad fish. You are swimming away from Jesus Christ. The net will be cast out in the last days. Jesus Christ will sort the good fish from the bad fish. The Holy Bible tells us a lot on this subject.

I am just trying to explain it my way. I am casting out my thoughts onto a bit of paper. I hope my short stories get you hooked on Jesus Christ. Do not spend your life swimming away from Jesus Christ. You could become a fisher of men for heaven's sake. I am one of the best fishermen around my local churches. I am always reeling people into a relationship with Jesus Christ. I became a fisher of men because I want to see lives being changed. My life was changed because Jesus Christ reeled me in. I lived by the sea and Jesus Christ called me to fish for the broken souls in your society.

22

The rudder on my ship in a storm

You cannot see the rudder on a ship. The rudder steers the ship in the direction you want it to go in. The rudder on my ship was not in my hands. My childhood steered me into violent storms. My family loved to commit crime. My birth father was addicted to drugs when I was born. I took the drugs like a mug. The rudder of drug addiction steered me into the storms of violence. My crimes sailed me into the prison system. What do kids do when they are born rudderless. Look at my story.

You will see what it does. My life battered me into a ship that refused to sink. You learn to drift through the storms of violence. I tried to make my ship lighter. I sailed away from my home. I was hoping that it would steer me onto a path of hope. Sailing away from my home broke my mother's heart.

Years of homelessness did not help me to find hope. Who is this man Jesus Christ? This man Jesus Christ became my rudder. Jesus Christ was trying to steer me onto a new path.

I resisted this new path. It became a battle on the high seas. I only sail in rough seas and Jesus Christ was taking me into a calm sea. I shouted out. I told Jesus Christ to steer me away from certain death. I now sit back, and I let Jesus Christ control the rudder on my ship. I can now write about the times when I was rudderless. I did not know any other life than prison and crime. I was shipwrecked more times than I care to remember. I can be foolish sometimes in my new life.

I said Jesus Christ let me put my hands on the rudder. I would have to write a short story about that time. Do you feel like you are sailing around rudderless in your sinful life? The world is your rudder my friend. The greed for material wealth will sail you away from Jesus Christ. Have a look at what is steering your rudder. I was rudderless in my life. I do not know what sails people to be successful and rich. A homeless person is just a rudderless ship in my eyes. The rudder is such a small part of a ship.

A two-foot rudder can steer a twenty-two-foot ship. Even mighty ships are controlled by a little rudder. I see people as ships. I want them to have a look at their rudders. The rudder of sin has the power to shipwreck any man. The rich and famous can find themselves shipwrecked. I want people to hand their rudders over to Jesus Christ. I want them to experience the feelings of amazing grace. You will sail in a calm sea of living waters. Do not think that it is all plain sailing with Jesus Christ.

The Apostle Paul handed his rudder over to Jesus Christ. What a story that is. Jesus Christ sailed the Apostle Paul into all sorts of storms. The joy of being in a storm for Jesus Christ is utterly amazing grace. I have been through the storms for Jesus Christ. My writing just flows because I am sitting by the sea. I must go back into the real world soon. Jesus Christ has his hands on my rudder so the world can wait on me. Why did Jesus Christ put me in the real world? I was free in my homeless years. The last ten years has taught me to trust Jesus Christ with my rudder.

23

A navigation system built into a ship

I like the old stories of the captains who sailed over the mighty sea. A ship can now sail around the world without the captain steering it. The ships have navigation systems built into them. I was lost at sea. I did not have a destination to my life. Most kids have stable homes. Their lives are mapped out for them. A good schooling sets a path to university. A career keeps them sailing in your material world. I did not have structure in my young life.

A life of crime sailed me into the prison system. Prison was my navigation system. Everything is set out for you in the prisons structure. Drifting through life without a destination was difficult. I could not live a life like other people. The other people are programmed by society. I now have a destination to my life. Jesus Christ is my destination. I long for the day when I see the face of Jesus Christ. I can still get lost in my life. It is hard to explain the promises of Jesus Christ. People are programmed by pride. Meeting Jesus Christ is the goal for me.

The promise of the Holy Spirit leads you into eternal life. We have a navigation system built into our souls. Every human has a longing to meet the creator of our universe. People search for the creator in many ways. I put my hands up. I tell Jesus Christ that I am not programmed by pride or greed. I was homeless for years, so my thinking is probably a bit weird. My navigation system tells me not to desire the things of your world. I do not let your world creep into my life.

I could be rich in man's pride. My navigation system takes me to church a dozen times a week. Learning about Jesus Christ keeps me sailing. It takes faith to let Jesus Christ reprogram you. I know that my destination is heaven. I would end up homeless if I were left to program my life. I would end up sailing myself into the prison system. Do you know that you have a built-in navigation system in your soul? Satan has you sailing in a material world. The things of this world could lead you to a place of torment.

I know that we will meet the God who created us. I believe that Jesus Christ is the Son of God. A homeless person is not destined to go anywhere in his life. A normal person is destined to prosper in your material world. Imagine if you were born into a drug infested council estate. You have no schooling or timetable to your life. Imagine if you had no one to guide you. That was my life when I was growing up. All I knew was crime and drugs. I ended up homeless for years.

I had no structure in my life. I longed for a prison sentence. You are given a number and a prison cell. You feel as if you belong to the prison system. Jesus Christ could be for you if you have no destination. Jesus Christ will reprogram the navigation system that is built into your soul. Do let the world lead you into a trap. You should be sailing through this life with Jesus Christ. Ask Jesus Christ to guide you away from your material world. Are you longing to meet the God who created you? Start your search by following Jesus Christ to the cross.

24

Finding a map for my life by the sea

How did we map the sea? The sea is so vast. What would we see if all the sea water were evaporated away? What would happen if all the coast lines joined up? Would it all fit like a jig saw? I am like a jigsaw. I am trying to fit the sea around my life. I am looking at maps today. Jesus Christ guides me in my writing. I did not have a map for my young life. I found Jesus Christ and he started to map out my life. My old life was not the map that I hoped for. Is there treasure in a map?

Jesus Christ is the treasure in my map. I will move mountains to find Jesus Christ. I stood by the waves of the sea. I cried out to Jesus Christ. I said my Lord I cannot see the map that you have for my life. Ten years on and I now see the map. I look to the sky today. I think is the universe mapped out above the sea. I am so imperfect when I am sitting on a sandy beach. Jesus Christ mapped out the sea before he thought about me. How did I find Jesus Christ without a paper map?

The Holy Spirit leads you to Jesus Christ. I was not looking for treasure in the sea when I was homeless. I was the treasure when I was homeless by the sea. No one came and showed me that Jesus Christ had a map for my life. Jesus Christ has a map for your life. You are just too selfish to follow it. You follow a map that is laden with material wealth. To trust that Jesus Christ will map out your life takes incredible faith. I have a faith that can move mountains.

It is not my writing. I just pour my ink on to my paper. I stood on this sandy beach ten years ago. A said my Lord this map is all new to me. I told my Lord that I was used to being homeless and free. Jesus Christ said my child I will show you where the treasure is. It is ten years on. I have found all the treasure that a sinful man can have. I did not find material treasure. I found the spiritual treasure. The Holy Bible is full of spiritual treasure. Would you like to have a map that is full of spiritual treasure?

Are you satisfied with your material treasure? Ask Jesus Christ to reveal the map for your life. It is not easy to follow a map that you cannot see. Ten years on and I am sitting at the sea. I look back on the last ten years. I can see the map that I followed. It was laden with joy and happiness. There was times of pain and sorrow. I never gave up on Jesus Christ. A lot of people find Jesus Christ. They start to follow a new map. They are full of joy. They are no longer following a heavenly map.

I watched these people. These people went back to searching the world. The world will give you imamate gratification. Following a new map changes your life. That is why people search the world for material wealth. I will sit here. I will look back on the last ten years with fond memories. I cannot see the next ten years. I will just trust the map that Jesus Christ has for my life. It will be tough going. I will sit here in ten years' time. I will look back again. I will always thank Jesus Christ because he mapped my life out. Are you looking for a new map to your life? Ask Jesus Christ to reveal the map that he has for your sinful life.

25

Anchoring the mountains down in the sea

God's mountains are peaking out of the mighty sea. The golden eagles are soaring around the peaks of God's mountains. Oh Lord let me soar on your heavenly winds with the golden eagles. The mountains are anchored down below the mighty sea. Oh Lord anchor my soul below the waves of your mighty sea. Oh Lord let my flesh reach the peaks of your snow-capped mountains. Oh Lord give me some slack so that I can soar with your golden eagles.

Oh Lord the waves are crashing against your snow-capped mountains. Oh Lord protect me from your violent sea. There is no mountain to high or low for me to see that Jesus Christ loves me. Oh Lord give me the faith to move your mountains out of this mighty sea. The mountains will rip themselves from their foundations when Jesus Christ returns in glory. The clouds are rapping themselves around my God's snow-capped mountains. Oh lord rap your forgiveness around my sinful flesh.

Jesus Christ surveys the sea from the peaks of God's mountains. Oh Lord bring me out of my deep sea of sin. Oh Lord I am longing to see your face. How far did my God stretch his sea? Oh Lord take me back to the peaks of your mountains. Oh Lord the golden eagles are surrounding me. Oh Lord I can feel their power in their awesome stretch. Their wings are feathered. Their beady eyes are on me. Oh Lord keep my sinful eyes on your amazing grace.

The mountains are beginning to shake with anger. Oh Lord shake my soul when I forget that I can climb a mountain to meet you. The mountains are bowing down before my Lord. Oh Lord I bow down before my sins come before your mighty throne. The mountains peaks are hidden from my sinful eyes. Oh Lord see that my sins are forgiven at your sons sacrifice on the cross. Oh Lord the sinners are running to the mountains side. Oh Lord I want to hide my sinful eyes under the waves of your sea.

The snow is fallen on the side of my God's mountains. Oh Lord I want to be snow white when your colourful son returns to judge this sinful world. The worlds sins will be exposed at the top of my God's mountains. That is my thoughts about my Jesus Christ. Would you climb my mountain to meet Jesus Christ? Your sins will be exposed when Jesus Christ returns to judge this sinful world. I have climbed a mountain with my Lord.

Some people are not prepared to climb a mountain for Jesus Christ. I felt the highs of being on a mountain with Jesus Christ. I felt the lows as I tried to hide my sins under the deep blue sea. I am anchored to my God's mountains. The waves of my sins have lashed me against the mountains. I am pleased with this short story. I know how to climb a mountain with Jesus Christ. I pray that you will find the faith to climb a mountain to meet Jesus Christ. You will experience the highs and the lows. We are called to climb a mountain for Jesus Christ. I have moved the mountains for you in this short story.

26

God's holy wind blowing your sails

I was sailing through my life on my own. I did not have a holy wind in my soul. I was just a homeless boy who lived by the sea. A holy wind blew in from the north. The holy wind changed the direction of my life. My sails where set in motion. Jesus Christ had promised me this holy wind. This holy wind blew me back up north. I was born in Scotland. I ran away to the seaside in England. The holy wind is like a breeze on a hot summer's day.

Why does this sinful world not want a holy wind from my loving God? God's holy wind could sail poverty into riches unseen by man's sinful eyes. The rich and famous are too proud to call out to my Jesus Christ. This holy wind will give you a wealth of knowledge. Let us look at the disciples of Jesus Christ. These men where fearless when Jesus Christ walked alongside them. Jesus Christ was crucified, and the disciples felt afraid. They laid Jesus Christ in an unknown tomb. The disciples huddled together in an upper room.

Mary went to the tomb weeping and wailing. Mary arrives to find out that the tomb is empty. Mary asked a man where my lord is. The man reply's and Mary fell at his feet. Read the Holy Bible and you will get the whole story. There are many accounts of what took place. Mary runs back to the fearful disciples. Mary tells them everything that happened. The dispels told Mary that she has lost her mind. They all wait, and they pray. Suddenly a figure appears in the upper room.

Read the Holy Bible and that will give you the whole picture. I only have one page to share my story. Doubting Thomas was missing from this event. Doubting Thomas will not believe. Jesus Christ appears to Thomas. Jesus Christ instructs the disciples to wait on the promise. The disciples are wiping their tears away. A rushing wind swept through the upper room. The Holy Spirit filled the disciples with a holy wind. Peter leads the disciples out into the streets of Jerusalem.

Thousands of people were filled with a holy wind. The place was on holy fire. The church was born out of that moment. Peter is heading to the temple and he spots a lame beggar. Peter looks him in the eyes and says gold or silver I do not have. Peter took the lame man by the hand. Peter said arise in the name of Jesus Christ. The man then danced with Peter to the temple. I was not lame when a man held my hand. I was a waste of space back then. I received a holy wind in my soul.

I then danced to a song. Amazing grace how sweet is the sound. The sound of a rushing wind swept through my soul. This sinless generation is trying to generate a holy wind from a material world. You know part of my story through my short stories. I believe in Jesus Christ. This holy wind is available to any man or woman. Some churches are trying to generate a holy wind with wild song and flashing lights. There were no flashing lights in the upper room. There were a bunch of fearful men and women. You must believe in Jesus Christ if you want to receive this holy wind in your soul.

27

My sea defence by the sea

I am walking along the shoreline. I can see a sea defence in front of me. I will rest here for this short story. What is this sea defence for? This sea defence is to stop the sea from reaching man's land. Man has claimed land from the sea. I do not think that man has any wright to claim land from the sea. The sea is drawing itself back in forth in anger. The mighty sea will claim its land back from man. I look at what defences I had as a child.

An angary drug infested council estate is just as angary as this sea. My family made my drug infested council estate angary. A child sees pain in that sinful drug infested council estate. My drug addiction led me into the depths of criminality. A life of crime and a ravaged body was my life. I robbed my drug infested council estate. I was robbed of a childhood. I robbed my own criminal family. I fought the good fight in my teenage years. My uncle was a coward and a bully. My family turned on me, so I lost that protection.

Every two-bob bit nobody wanted me dead. I was a bloody mess in my young life. The cowards and bullies put a contract on my head. The cowards and bullies could not take a contract out on a mobile phone. No one got paid for stabbing me up. I was just a teenager and I ran away from home. My twenties were spent as a runaway. I found myself reaching thirty years old. Jesus Christ came into my life. I will declare that Jesus Christ is my defence in your dark world.

Jesus Christ raised me up from the dirty ground. The baseball bats and knifes could not reach me in my newfound faith. There is a spiritual battle in your sinful world. I do not seek revenge on the cowards who tried to murder my love. No one can kill the love that I have for Jesus Christ. I have prayer and a fighting spirit. I am a gangster for Jesus Christ. The cowards push darkness and I push back with my light. My heart sings songs of forgiveness not hatred. We all need a sea defence against the darkness.

I can see a bit of anger in my writing today. I will pause for a moment. I just prayed to my Jesus Christ. I said Lord do not let hatred enter my heart. Let us carry on writing about my life. I have wanted revenge over the years. I will not let Satan turn me into a bully. I have never been a bully. I have my Jesus Christ, so I can pray for the cowards and bully's. I can see that they are empty inside. Look at your own life today. Do you need a sea defence against the darkness of sin?

My Jesus Christ will protect you. The waves of bitterness and anger cannot reach you when you believe. I really did have a hard life. I found the sea so there will be no more tears about my past. The last ten years have made up for my lost years in a drug infested council estate. We all need to defend ourselves in our lives. Ask Jesus Christ to put a spiritual sea defence around your soul. The waves of fear cannot reach you when you believe in Jesus Christ. I must have a spiritual sea defence when I enter your dark sinful world.

28

Cliffs overlooking the sea

I was stuck in a violent sea. I could not see a way out. I was surrounded by cliffs. That is how I describe my drug addiction. I ran away from home and I lived by the sea. Isolation was my best friend. I thought that I would die in a sea of blood. I looked to the top of the cliffs. A faint light was flickering in the night. I was being drawn to climb up the cliffs face. I swam towards the cliffs. I noticed that Jesus Christ was standing on the cliffs. I started to climb up the cliffs face.

I saw the face of Jesus Christ and it was all too bright for my sinful eyes. I threw myself back into my stormy sea. I swam away from the light of the world. The promise of forgiveness was not for me. I was not worthy enough to receive Jesus Christ as my savour. I swam in every direction. The light got brighter. My arms tired. I found myself at the bottom of the cliffs. Jesus Christ was shining a pathway up the cliffs face. I watched other people escaping their drug addiction.

They found a way up the cliffs face. They did not last long in the real world. They were tossed back into a sea of drug addiction. They had found self-worth and they lost it all. I never had self-worth. I did not want it. I would rather not taste self-worth if it meant losing it again. Would Jesus Christ keep me on top of the cliffs. I had to find my trust. This story is written this way for a reason. I was never a part of your

66

world. I was homeless by the sea. I hope you can see my sense in this short story.

I climbed the cliffs face to meet Jesus Christ. Jesus Christ never leaves you or forsakes you. I did not want self-worth because I know that I am worth so much more to Jesus Christ. So much worth that he took the nails on the cross for my sins. Jesus Christ called his disciples on a sandy beach. Jesus Christ would have walked down to the sandy beach. Where did Jesus Christ walk down from? A cliff face or a hill. Jesus Christ met me on a sandy beach.

Jesus Christ took me by the hand. Jesus Christ led me up the cliffs face. I stood on top of the cliff with the light of the world. Jesus Christ pointed down into the sea. I looked down. I saw a red sea. People where drowning in flames of red. I look around your society and that is what I see today. People are drowning depression. People are surrounded by cliffs. I said Jesus Christ we have to save these sinners. Jesus Christ said you go my dear child. I said lord I cannot go at it alone.

Jesus Christ said there is a helper. Remember the upper room in my other short story. I have never lost that picture of a red sea. I have been pulling people out of the red sea for ten years. It is an amazing story. I do not boast about what I have done. The Holy Spirit has shined a light on my path for ten years. I followed the map my friends. Jesus Christ is my lighthouse on top of the cliffs. I sometimes think that I would get locked up in a mental hospital for writing my short stories. Are you looking for a lighthouse in your dark nights? Are you brave enough to climb up the cliffs face?

29

Lost at sea in a spiritual storm

Jesus Christ guides me when I lose direction in my life. I have got lost a few times over the last ten years. I asked Jesus Christ witchwhich direction he had taken me in. Think of ship that is going into a harbour. Jesus Christ was drawing me out into a stormy sea. Other ships were making their way into a harbour. Jesus Christ led me into an open sea, and I felt all alone. Do you feel like you have lost all hope in your life? Do not be afraid I always find my way back to the harbour.

I asked Jesus Christ why he left me in a stormy sea. The storm passed and I asked Jesus Christ why he had left me. Jesus Christ said that he was with me in the storm. Jesus Christ said that he was at the captain's wheel. There is a passage in the Holy Bible. Jesus Christ has drawn my attention to it. The disciples where in a storm with Jesus Christ. A storm overwhelmed the boat. Jesus Christ stood up and he rebuked the storm for his disciples. I asked the Lord why I had to go through the whole storm on my own.

I said Jesus Christ why did you not rebuke my loss. I said a loved one has been ripped out of my heart. I lost a dear mother at such a young age. Jesus Christ said that he could not wipe my tears away because he was at the captain's wheel of my ship. I wanted to bail out of my ship in the beginning.

I had to deal with the grief of losing my dear mother. The drugs had suppressed my grief for years. I had to deal with this in my later years with Jesus Christ.

Do you feel like that Jesus Christ has abandoned you in a storm of grief? Look to the captain's wheel. Jesus Christ never leaves or forsakes us. I never noticed that Jesus Christ was at the captain's wheel. I came through the tears and fears. I dealt with the pain of losing my dear mother. People are lost in this sinless world. I must lead the broken people to the light of the world. Some people do not see the lighthouse on the cliffs. I have been a beacon of hope to the people that are lost in a sea of grief.

I have counselled people who are coming of drugs. All the feelings come back, and they feel afraid. Some of them cannot deal with it and they return to a stormy sea. I am lucky because I love Jesus Christ. I have one of the saddest stories. I also have one of the greatest stories in the last ten years. I am now sharing the last ten years in a book of short stories. Every story has been written at a different time in my life. There are more short stories to come.

Take your time as you read them and enjoy them. I recommend that you read two stories a week. Give them time to sink in. Seek Jesus Christ in-between reading my short stories. You maybe feel lost in your life. We have a destination to our lives. Heaven is open to the people who will believe in Jesus Christ. I was lost and Jesus Christ found me just in time. That is me done for today. I have another short story for my collection. I must go back into the real world. I will see the homeless beggars on the streets. I know that they are lost to Jesus Christ. I will share this short story with some of them.

30

Keeping your head above the waves of the sea

I had some strength to keep my head above the waves. I was drowning since the day I was born. I was raised around storms of untold pain. Waves of violence threatened to drown me in my teenage years. My head was dropping below the waves of the sea. I was left dripping in blood. I ran away from my pain. I found myself alone by this beautiful sea. This beautiful sea could not hold my pain. My head was dropping below the waves again. I heard a voice standing on the waves of my pain.

The voice said reach out your hands my dear child. I reached my hands out just in time. I stood on the waves of my pain with my Jesus Christ. Are you keeping your head above the waves of the red sea? Do you smile at your friends and family? Do they see you walking on the waves of the sea? Are you pretending that you are ok with your hidden tears? To many people appear to walk on the waves of the sea. They are really sinking into a red sea of pain. I am such a caring person in my life.

I have spoken with people behind closed doors. I see their tears and fears. The world sees a false happiness. I see their true pain. I have learned a lot over the last ten years. Jesus Christ stood on the waves of the sea and he called a disciple from a boat. The dispels stepped on to the waves of the sea. The disciple took his eyes of Jesus Christ and he started to sink into the waves. The disciple cried out to Jesus Christ. Jesus Christ reached out to the drowning disciple.

The story is in the Holy Bible. Have a read of it tonight. You can google it on your smart phone. The passage is short, but it is powerful. I know people who once had a faith in Jesus Christ. They were walking on the waves with Jesus Christ. They took their eyes of Jesus Christ and they sank into the red sea. So many people have their eyes fixed on the world. Your sinful eyes want to lust after material things. The world is a distraction. My eyes are fixed on Jesus Christ. I sit at the sea and the world is behind me.

I will enter your world. My eyes will wonder everywhere. A long-legged blond in a skirt will have me panting like a dog. The beer garden will tempt me to sit a while with a long-legged blond. I keep my eyes to the sky. This world wants me below the waves of the sea. Why did Jesus Christ put me in a world of temptation? I was free by this sea in my homeless years. I watched sunsets in my homeless years. This sinful world is the reason that your head is dropping below the waves of the sea.

Oh lord keep my eyes fixed on you. Oh lord do not let my lustful eyes wonder over a long-legged blond in a beer garden. I must pray if I want to walk with Jesus Christ on the waves of the sea. Try taking your eyes away from the sinful world. You will see Jesus Christ standing on the waves of your pain. My eyes have wondered a thousand times over the last ten years. I have found myself crying out like the disciple. Jesus Christ always reaches his hands out to me. That is why I love Jesus Christ with all my heart and soul.

31

Roll back a spiritual sea with Jesus Christ

Oh Lord please roll back the waves of your mighty sea. Let us sinful people see that you are near to our tears. Oh Lord we are standing at the water's edge. Are your hidden sins trapped under the waves of the sea? Oh Lord roll back our layers and reveal our guilty sins before your father's throne. Our sins are like the salt from the sea. Oh Lord we are used to the taste of our salty sins. We cry saltwater tears in the night. The moon glisten on the surface of the sea.

The moon is like a clock for the sea. The moon draws the waves back and forth. Jesus Christ is pulling our lives apart. We walk on the sandy beach. The tide turns towards us. We run to a rockpool in fear of the Lord. The clouds evaporate the salt water from the rockpools. We are left hiding under a rock. Does this sound like you? I was hiding from Jesus

Christ. I was ashamed of my life in homelessness. The Holy Spirit fell upon me. Jesus Christ rolled my life back. I could not look at my past in the light of Jesus Christ.

Why would Jesus Christ roll my life back like the tides of the sea. It is because he loves me. I just did not love myself when I was a homeless drug addict. Society judged me in my homelessness. Jesus Christ loved me in my stubbornness. I refused to leave my seaside. I did not want to live in your judgemental society. I am rolling my life back for your society. My hard life left me loveless on your streets. People in society are living in a false sense of reality.

They are too scared to roll out their past sins to the eyes of Jesus Christ. Is the tide of the sea hiding all your guilty sins? Are you walking in pride with your family and friends? Every sin will be revealed before God's throne. The seas will be evaporated. You will be left naked and ashamed. Your sins will be exposed on the oceans floor. You will be ashamed of your sins. You will look to hide in a shell on the oceans floor. I roll back my thoughts and they frighten me. The times that I looked at a woman with lust with be exposed.

I cannot hide my lustfulness on the oceans floor. The feelings of anger and revenge will be exposed. I do not fear. I let Jesus Christ roll my life back. I have been declared not guilty because I confessed every sin. I laid my sins bare before the cross. I wanted to destroy the bullies and cowards. The people who hurt me are lucky because I found Jesus Christ. The society that judged me in my homeless years is going to be judged.

Every human on this earth will stand before God's throne.

Every human in society will have to give an account of their sins. I have tried to roll the sea back in prayer for you. Roll your own life back and confess your sins before the cross. The Holy Bible tells us that we have sinful eyes. It has taken me years to roll my life out before Jesus Christ. It has been painful, and I have shed tears. Just look at me now. I can sit here with my pen and paper. I am finished for today. I will leave this seaside. I will enter your sinful world. Oh Lord protect my sinful eyes so that I will not sin against you.

32

The roaring sea in a spiritual storm

The red sea is raging against my sinful flesh. I am trying to follow the creator of the mighty sea. The waves are rolling me over in my sinful flesh. The currents of guilt are trying to pull me away from the creator of the mighty sea. I will be swept away in a river of regrets. I am raging against my sinful flesh. My red blood is boiling up in my veins. I stand in a rage at the rugged cross. Why have you taken my loved ones away? I stand alone without friends.

I picked the rugged cross and my friends deserted me. I changed my life at the foot of the rugged cross. I found forgiveness and my old enemies are raging at me. I forgive them for the hurt they caused me in the red sea. No one wants to except me with a rugged cross on my back. I tried to go back to my old life by the sea. I wanted to find my old friends and enemies away from the rugged cross. It is so hard for me to stand at the rugged cross. The red sea is raging on one side. The rugged cross is standing on the other side.

Is Jesus Christ mad at me for running away from the rugged cross. Oh, forgive me Lord. I did run away from the rugged cross. Does Jesus Christ shed a tear with me? I lost my old enemies and friends because I stood at the rugged cross. I do not look back away more. The red sea is behind me. The rugged cross is a head of me. The waves of anger are stilled when I sit at the rugged cross. I cannot pull my old enemies and friends towards the cross.

Bribing people with my time and money is fruitless. They are blind to the rugged cross. Jesus Christ shed his blood to draw them out of the red sea. The crowds where shouting in a rage two thousand years ago. Crucify Jesus Christ and leave us at the mercy of the red sea. The people of Jerusalem shouted out in pure hatred. Jesus Christ was hanging on the old, rugged cross. They laid Jesus Christ in a tomb. Jesus Christ rose again to save the people who had crucified him. The red sea is raging today. People are in despair.

Everyone seems to fear the rugged cross. I do not fear because I picked the old, rugged cross over my old life in sin. I stood on a cliff and I overlooked the red sea. The pain and horror are in the eyes of my old enemies. The red sea is tossing people around in fear. Oh Lord why did I pick the old, rugged cross over the red sea. Is the red sea raging against your sins. Are you being tossed around in a sea of fear? I have been there in my darkest days.

I am now free because I stand at the rugged cross. I am sitting by the sea today. I have written a few short stories in a few days. I normally try and write one or two a week. I think Jesus Christ is speaking to your sinful world. I will write these short stories for Jesus Christ because I believe. Do not spend your whole life in the red sea. You must choose the rugged cross if you want to escape the red sea. It is not easy to choose the rugged cross. You can see that in my short stories. I picked the old, rugged cross ten years ago. Would you choose the old, rugged cross over a selfish life in the red sea?

33
A rainbow appearing over the sea

I watched hundreds of rainbows appearing over the sea. My homeless years were spent under the rainbows. The rainbow rain would fall on me. The colours would appear in an arch. Everyone sees a rainbow in the sky. Few people have watched a rainbow appearing over the sea. The light rain tells me that a rainbow will appear in the sky. The arch would appear, and my heart would break. My bleary eyes watched the rainbows in the sky. The colours would melt my tears away.

I did not have any colour in my cheeks. The drugs left me skinny and pale grey. I would rub my eyes with my hands. I felt that my cheek bones where popping through my skin.

My starvation stripped my flesh to the bone. I knew that it was time for a prison sentence. The police were always after me. That is why I hid by the sea. I would get a sentence from a judge. I would find myself in a grey prison cell. I would go cold turkey in a grey cell. Sleepless nights made my sentence longer.

I would look in the mirror after a few weeks. The colour of health would return to my cheeks. I would smile as my cheek bones disappeared. The prison food gave me chubby cheeks. The rays of the sun in the exercise yard brought a smile to my rosy cheeks. I enjoyed the prison life in my teenage years. The days where long. The nights became peaceful. You would find yourself coming to the end of your sentence. I was cast out of prison.

I would be homeless again. I had no family or friends, so I returned to my seaside. I took the drugs to numb the pain of loneliness. The fat would fade away in my starvation. I would rub my eyes. My cheek bones would remind me of my past. I had no mirror in my homelessness, so I never seen my pale face. Once again, I would be looking at the rainbows appearing over the sea. I prayed out a thousand times. I never heard a word from God. I found myself in a church. A man prayed for me. A rainbow of colours landed in my soul.

I heard a soft voice deep inside my soul. The voice said it is I your Lord. I closed my eyes. I ran away from the rainbow of colours in my soul. I was confused about this man praying for me. I could handle a dull prison cell. I could not handle a rainbow of colours in my soul. I could not outrun Jesus Christ, so I accepted him as my rainbow. I told the world that

Jesus Christ was God's most colourful son. I laid my hands on the poor. I prayed for the poor. I saw the poor bursting into a rainbow of colours.

I could see that sparkle in their eyes. I noticed that other people where dull. I then heard how they judged the poor. You will be forever dull if you judge the poor. This short story has me crying happy tears. I was a bit angary when I wrote my last two short stories. It is funny how things change in a matter of weeks. I have not picked up my pen for a few weeks. I am glad that I picked it up today. I am sitting at the sea. There is a hint of colour in the sky. I will finish here because a rainbow may appear in the sky above me.

34

Stillness on the surface of the sea

The disciples of Jesus Christ are stuck in a stormy sea. Jesus Christ raised his hands and the sea obeyed. The disciples said who is this man. They had seen Jesus Christ taming the violent sea. I am blessed by this story in my life. My once violent sea was tamed by Jesus Christ. I lived alone by the sea. I watched the storms at night. The thunder roared over the sea. I thought that my life was going to end in sorrow. The drugs stopped working. The waves were lashing me in the night.

The morning brought a clearer view. A violent storm is

raging over your sinful dryland. Wars are raging. Spiritual poverty is killing sinners. There is no stillness on this barren dryland. Sinners are thirsting for living waters. The spiritual battle goes unseen by sinful eyes. Jesus Christ never roared at the storm. Jesus Christ whispered without stretched arms. Jesus Christ was to find himself on an old, rugged cross. His arms were stretched out and he never roared out. Jesus Christ whispered with a soft voice.

Jesus Christ said it is finished. A mental health crisis is washing itself over this barren dryland. Jesus Christ can bring stillness to this sinful dryland. I used to lay on a bench in my homeless years. The guilt of running away from home was like the lighting in the sky. There is now a stillness in my hands. I can sit and write my short stories for Jesus Christ. Are you looking for stillness in your sinful life? Oh Lord bring peace to this barren dryland.

Oh Lord let your voice be heard through my short stories. Jesus Christ whispered from an old, rugged cross. I am crying from the top of my voice in this short story. There are no rainbows in the sky today. The clouds are dark. The waves are rolling in towards me. I have the faith to raise my hands over this untamed sea. I do not have the faith to raise my hands over your barren dryland. Jesus Christ could calm the storms on your barren dryland. The sinners are too proud to call on the name of my Jesus Christ.

This sinful generation would be shouting out like they did two thousand years ago. Oh Lord bring some stillness into my writing. I have lived in peace with God for the last ten years. I do not fear God. I sit at the foot of an old, rugged cross. What would you give to have a stillness in your soul? Stop running around like a headless chicken. The Holy Bible tells us to be still In the presence of the Lord. I love the stillness of writing my short stories.

The world behind me is living in a storm of mental health. I look out to the sea. I pray for the sinners with mental health. People's minds are lusting after worldly things. I am lusting after Jesus Christ in my writing. Take yourself out of the noisy world. You will find perfect peace by the sea. The disciples found peace when Jesus Christ rebuked the storm. I love that passage in the Holy Bible. What fear did the disciples feel as their boat was being tossed around in a stormy sea. What peace did they feel when Jesus Christ raised his hands over the storm? Jesus Christ can bring peace into your troubled mind.

35
A glistening path on the surface of the sea

I used to lay on a bench by the sea. I would look up into a dark sky. The dark sky would be carrying my guilt and shame. The rain would fall on me. The sky would appear a little lighter. I would wait on the moment that I treasured most. It took a little while before a seen something special.

The clouds would split apart. A ray of sunshine would shine on the ocean's surface. This is a special day. I have company. I am sitting by the sea with my daughter. You see I ran away from a three-year-old child.

I found Jesus Christ and he reunited me with a fifteen-year-old daughter. My daughter has lived with me for the last ten years. I am no longer a homeless teenager. I am sitting in my car teaching my daughter about the sea. I tell my daughter to keep her eyes on the dark sky. A light rain is falling on my cars wind screen. We sit and chat for a while. The clouds are starting to split. The suns light has pierced the surface of the sea. A glistening path makes its way to the shoreline.

The clouds are now bristling in colours. My daughter's eyes light up in delight. She has been lusting after Jesus Christ for the last ten years. My daughter says that it looks like a ladder. My daughter said the ladder could lead us to heavens front door. She says it all with a mystery in her young eyes. I can now see things with clear eyes. I can time the moment when the sun splits the dark clouds. My daughter is taking pictures on her phone. This world is too fast.

People are too busy to search the sea for such a sight. This is a sight that my daughter will remember for the rest of her life. My life was timeless when I was homeless by the sea. I sometimes yearn to be free again. I have not spent the last ten years on my own. My daughters mother grew up in the same place as me. She sadly died when my daughter was twelve years old. My daughters mother never escaped the red sea. My daughter went off the rails at a young age.

I was reunited with her when she was fifteen. She has lived

in England with me since then. I used to live under the dark clouds in my homelessness. Jesus Christ broke through to my dull life. In the same way the physical sun just broke through the dark clouds. Jesus Christ left a glistening path in my way. Me and my daughter have walked along the glistening path for the last ten years. There were times when the clouds of fear darkened our path.

We kept walking in faith and Jesus Christ would break through with his light. Are you looking at dark clouds of fear in your life? I pray that Jesus Christ will break through with his light. Sometimes we must walk through the valley of death. Depression can hang over me for weeks at a time. I enjoy them dark times. I know that Jesus Christ will break through the dark clouds of my depression. I know people who never found God's light through the dark clouds. Their lives ended in suicide. I pray that Jesus Christ will break through your dark clouds of fear. Do you see a glisten path in my short stories?

36

Finding a spiritual harbour in the storms

I am sailing through my life. My main goal is to reach a harbour of amazing grace. The sea is stormy today. Jesus

Christ is calling me into a harbour of amazing grace. The Holy Spirits wind will propel me over the waves of fear. I see beyond the fears of others. I keep my eyes on heavens harbour. Some people will not put their sails up for Jesus Christ. Some people want a harbour of worldly wealth. A harbour of wealth will keep your flesh safe in this life.

A spiritual harbour of amazing grace will keep your soul afloat for an eternity. I have found a spiritual harbour of amazing grace. I have rested there with Jesus Christ. I do not stay in a harbour of amazing grace all the time. Jesus Christ asks me to go out into the stormy red sea. I am resting on a bench by the sea. This is like a harbour of amazing grace for me. The world behind me is the stormy red sea. I know that people are drowning behind me. Homeless people are sleeping on the streets. Some people with homes live in isolation.

I have been living in the real world for ten years. Who would I be if I could not escape to my harbour of amazing grace? How do people survive in the big city's? I went to London about six years ago. I did not like the big city. The buildings were high. The streets where busy. I had a panic attack, and I went back home. I ran to the sea and I felt so free. I renamed the sea to a harbour of amazing grace. I used to call it my resting place. Do you feel trapped in a dark world?

Are you sailing around rudderless? Find your harbour of amazing grace because you will become a shipwreck for sure. Put your sails up. Ask Jesus Christ to blow his holy wind into your soul. Give Jesus Christ the captains wheel and he will guide you into a harbour of amazing grace. I could go on and on about a harbour of amazing grace. I could tell you how peaceful it is. Faith will take your soul into your harbour of amazing grace. I look around this dark world.

Ninety five percent of people are happy with their harbours of material wealth. Five percent of the people are drowning in the red sea. They are crying out for a harbour of amazing grace. It is my job to show them the way. I have taken a lot of people to the church. They were all in the five percent bracket. I got to know some of the nighty five percent of people. They were materially commutable in life. You get a better picture when you look behind the curtains.

Some of these people are not satisfied with themselves. They are no different to the homeless beggars. We all long for rest. I was a tormented soul when I was homeless. Jesus Christ crossed the sea of galilee to reach a tormented soul. Jesus Christ healed the tormented man with a few words. The man then rested in his harbour of amazing grace. Jesus Christ is calling you into a harbour of amazing grace. I am trying my hardest to show that in my personal story. Another short story completed by the sea. I am now going to walk into the red sea. I will walk into your dark world and I will declare my love for Jesus Christ.

37

God's love is as deep as the sea

His love is as deep as the sea. His sacrifice on the cross is as wide as the sea. No creature below the sea has been formed without thought to its needs. The mountains are anchored down in his teachings. The beloved disciples are being tossed around in a storm. The disciples said Jesus Christ do you not care. The disciples told Jesus Christ that they were going to perish at the work of his hands. Jesus Christ raises his hands up in the air.

The hands of Jesus Christ filled the sea with water. Only the creator can control his own creation. Jesus Christ showed his love to a world that was crying saltwater tears. His love never turns on you. His tides can be counted to roll in and out. Jesus Christ placed the moon over the sea. The moon is a clock for the sea. We run away from his love on the cross. We are like a horse that is running along the waves of the sea. The horse's rider is seated high. He is ready to judge the world with his sword. We swim under the waves of lustfulness.

The waves will rage against our lustfulness. The currents of guilt will pull us away from a sea of forgiveness. We only want ten percent of his love. Man has only explored ten percent of the oceans floor. We are frightened to give ten percent of our love to the one who created the sea. I am not frightened to reveal my needs to the sea. I am writing this short story for the people who do not know about God's love on a cross. I love Jesus Christ more than a hundred percent.

My love for Jesus Christ goes deeper than the sea. Oh Lord take us deeper into the heart of your sea. Oh Lord take us to the corners of the deep see. Oh Lord show the sinners that you love them. The world behind me will not accept the love that hanged on an old, rugged cross. Where else can you find a love that is so sure. The sort of love that takes us to the unseen places. The disciples knew that Jesus Christ loved them more than the deep sea. Jesus Christ loved one dispels more than the other eleven.

It cannot be fair to love one disciple more than the others. The love of Jesus Christ does go deeper. We can never measure God's love by the depths of the sea. We can measure God's love on an old, rugged cross. The cross separated Jesus Christ from his father. Jesus Christ cried out, father why have you forsaken me at this hour. God would have told Jesus Christ that it was to save a soul like me. I love Jesus Christ because he saved my life. I would have died on the streets for sure.

I was not happy about leaving my sea behind. I have shown people my love for Jesus Christ. Some of them think that I am crazy for loving Jesus Christ. These people do not know my past. I think that it is crazier that Jesus Christ would love me. I have not been perfect over the last ten years. Loving Jesus Christ washes over my imperfectness. Jesus Christ will love you more if you are imperfect. I am just loving my Jesus Christ today. I sit in my harbour of amazing grace and I get to write about his love.

38

Burying our heads in the sand

What fool sticks his head in the sand? The fool will miss the beauty of a setting sun. I was no fool in my homeless years. I watched the sun setting itself over the sea. I want to tell you about all its wonders. My homelessness had me buried under the sand. My head was popping out of the sand. I never missed the beauty of the sun setting itself over the sea. A lot of people had their heads buried in the sand. I see God's true grace in a setting sun. The sun and sea brought tears to my eyes.

The sun and sea could make me feel imperfect in my homeless years. Man's eyes are darkened in his sinful nature. Man's eyes are colour blind to God's true nature. The sinful man forgets that he is created more beautiful than a setting sun. I looked dirty in my homeless years. I felt it when the sun said its goodbyes to my eyes. I never buried my head in the sand. I was free to gaze at the sky. I watched the sky as it was bristling in colours. A bright orange circle caught my sinful eyes.

I was looking for the reasons to my sinful life. Other people were burying their heads in the dirty sand. I always prayed to God when a sun was setting itself over the sea. I heard a soft voice in my soul. It said that there was something greater than a setting sun. Behold my friends because God revealed something. This something was more beautiful than a perfect setting sun. Jesus Christ dazzled the world two thousand years ago.

God placed the physical sun in the sky, and he placed his only begotten son in a manger. Jesus Christ grew into a man. This man dazzled the world with parables. The parables revealed the secrets of God's eternal grace. Sinful men heard the voice of Jesus Christ and they ran away. They buried their heads in the sand because Jesus Christ spoke with the authority of heaven and earth. The sinful men plotted together a plan. The sinful men said that they must crucify the Messiah. God's only begotten son was brighter than the physical sun.

Jesus Christ brought the colours of a sunset into the souls of the poor. The sinful men hatched their plan. Jesus Christ was left hanging on an old, rugged cross. The sky grew dark. The sinful men looked away from God's cross. There was no sunset in the sky when Jesus Christ breathed his last breath. One man looked at the cross and he fell to his knees. The man said surly he was the only begotten son of God. Another man was on his way into Jerusalem.

The man spotted Jesus Christ on the cross. This man took the body of Jesus Christ. The man laid him in an unknown tomb. The disciples of Jesus Christ had deserted him. They all huddled together in an upper room. Jesus Christ was no longer with them. The disciples wait on the promise. The Holy Spirit fell on the disciples. The disciples burst into the colours of God's setting sun. Have you got your head stuck in the sand? You are missing out on the wonders of Jesus Christ. I did not bury my head in the sand. I found Jesus Christ in a sunset.

39

Finding treasure in a spiritual sea

I was homeless for years. I lived by the sea. I did not have any treasure in my pockets. I looked extremely poor when I was homeless. Sleeping in the open air left me cold. I wanted a home to warm my weary soul. No one tells a homeless teenager that he is richer than the fools with a home. I never searched for gold or silver in my homeless years. I begged on the streets for copper change. People would look at me with disgust. Some people did throw me their loose change.

I few people would smile at me on a cold day. Only the brave would call me a scumbag to my face. Someone did call me a scumbag on a cold day. I stood up and I ranted about my sinful life. I now look back at what treasure these people had. They looked down on me as I sat begging for loose change. I see wealth in their clothes. My clothes where rags to their eyes. I see pride in their walk. I walked back to my resting place with tears in my eyes. I found myself reaching thirty years old.

I had no treasure at thirty years old. I heard a soft voice inside my dirty soul. The voice said that I was to look under the sea. I could not see under the sea until Jesus Christ fell on me. A treasure of spiritual wealth landed on my knees. I was always on my knees when I prayed to God. The heavenly treasure started to overwhelm my eyes. Has anyone seen the treasures that Jesus Christ promised me? I closed my eyes, and I ran away.

I was not worthy enough to receive heavenly treasure in my homeless state. The voice in my soul said that I was worthy enough to know Jesus Christ. Why is the world seeking treasures in material wealth? Material treasure will only rob you of life. Heavenly treasure gives life to your broken soul. This sinful world cannot feel the heavenly treasure. The spiritual treasure comes in one name. Jesus Christ was the treasure under the sea. Rust cannot destroy the treasures that come from heaven.

Heavenly treasure is purer than gold. Heavenly treasure is sweeter than honey. The laws of gravity cannot explain its meaning. Wisdom cannot grasp its deeper meaning. The long grasses on a sand dune sway side to side. We cannot see the wind that moves the grasses to dance. We hear the grasses rustling in the wind. We cannot hear the God who blows the wind. The disciples of Jesus Christ were trapped in an upper room. A mighty rushing wind swept through the upper room.

The dispels started to dance like the grasses on a sand dune. The dispels received the spiritual treasures. Jesus Christ promised the disciple's his spiritual treasure. Are you feeling spiritually poor in your life? Does your material treasure leave you feeling empty? There are treasures to be found in Jesus Christ. I am still materially poor, but my writing is the treasure from heaven. My short stories are for the sinners who are spiritually poor. I have shared my spiritual treasure with the poor. This spiritual treasure glistens in your eyes.

Would you give up your material treasure for spiritual treasure.

40

Carrying unwanted cargo on your ship

I see myself as a ship in the eyes of God. I was sailing through my teenage years in homelessness. I carried all my cargo on my back. The guilt of running away from my home weighed heavy in my soul. My guilt was sinking me deeper in to the red sea. I found Jesus Christ and he wanted to take my unwanted cargo. The power of the Holy Spirit lightened my ship. I was scared when the Holy Spirit lifted my guilt. I ran away and I filled my ship up again. I was not so trusting in this Holy Spirit.

The world loaded me with shame. Begging on the streets brought me to tears. I was looked down on when I was homeless. My ship was laden down with a drug addiction. I found my trust and Jesus Christ lightened my ship again. I notice that other people are carrying unwanted cargo. Sinful men have ships laden with material wealth. I know believers who are heavy ships. They go to the church on a Sunday. A few good songs will lighten their ships for a while.

Their Sunday dinner tastes better after a few good songs.

These people start their Mondays with a smile. The weight of the world returns on a Monday night. They are then sinking in the week. I am smarter than the average believer. I know how to keep my ship light in the week. I sail myself to bible study on a Monday night. I am then sailing through Tuesday with a breeze in my sails. Tuesday night communion lets me unload my shame. I could carry on explaining my week.

I serve Jesus Christ in the week. Are you carrying unwanted cargo on your ship? Are you sinking into the red sea? Jesus Christ took your unwanted cargo on an old, rugged cross. I know people who struggle to get through a day. They feel heavy and burdened by life itself. I now sail through my life. Your world does not hold me down. I have seen people losing their cargo of problems. They end up singing and dancing. Jesus Christ took their unwanted cargo.

I watched the weight returning to their souls. They became selfish with their newfound weight. They started to judge the people who were laden down with shame. I never judge the ships that are sinking in depression. I pray with them. I help them to understand the promises of Jesus Christ. I was a heavy ship many years ago. A man prayed for me and the weight disappeared. I was singing and dancing to the tune of amazing grace. I was as light as a butterfly in the wind.

I put my sails up. God's holy wind propelled me over the waves of my fears. I wish I had the space to tell you all the stories in my life. My daughter was a heavy ship in her young life. Something happened a few years ago. She put her hands out. She said Jesus Christ take all my unwanted cargo. My daughter sang and danced like a butterfly in the wind. The weight returned to her shoulders. I taught her everything I know. You must keep on giving Jesus Christ your unwanted cargo. I am sitting by the sea today. I am unloading my ship by writing this short story. Give Jesus Christ your unwanted cargo.

41

Jesus Christ throwing me a life jacket

I needed a life jacket from the moment I was born. I was destined to be drowning from birth. A was born into a drug infested council estate. A sea of drug addiction and violence does not give you a life jacket. I started to swim in crime. I abused every substance known to man. Prison only took you in for shelter. Prison was a time to build yourself up. The prison tossed me back on to the streets. Swimming against a tide of violence only draws blood from your flesh.

The blood does not give you a life jacket. Jesus Christ is the only person who cared for me. The Lord of the heavens and earth threw me a life jacket. I reached my hands out to Jesus Christ. I received a spiritual life jacket. The feeling of I do not belong in the red sea brought me to tears. A man was once drowning the physical sea. A passer-by spotted the man in distress. He phoned for the lifeguards. The lifeguards took to the sea. They spotted the man in the water and they threw him a life jacket.

The sea was stormy, and the ten-foot waves rocked the boat back and forth. The man in the water was safe because he had his life jacket. The lifeboat crew manage to drag him aboard their boat. They rapped the man in warm blankets. That man was forever grateful to the lifeguards. I am like the man who got rescued. I am forever grateful. I always thank Jesus Christ from the bottom of my heart. Are you being tossed around in a stormy sea?

Would you reach your hands out for a spiritual life jacket? Jesus Christ is offering you a spiritual life jacket. We all need a spiritual life jacket for our souls. I always felt a bit vulnerable when I was growing up. I grew up around a lot of bad stuff. I was always drowning in my life. I am not vulnerable today because I wear a spiritual life jacket. Your dryland represents a spiritual sea. I know that people are drowning in some sort of pain. Why are they to afraid to reach their hands out for a spiritual life jacket.

Some people will spend their whole lives drowning in depression. They will meet Jesus Christ when their flesh dies. They will ask Jesus Christ why he left them to drown in such sorrows. Jesus Christ will point to the spiritual life jacket. People will see an old, rugged cross. They will say that is not a life jacket. Do you see the old, rugged cross as a spiritual life jacket? The cross of Jesus Christ keeps my soul afloat. Some people are too stubborn to look at the cross.

Their material wealth is their life jacket in this sinful world. A material life jacket will keep your flesh afloat in this life. I want to reach out to the people who do not have a material life jacket. These people recognize that their souls are drowning in a red sea of pain. Drop your material life jacket and reach out to the old, rugged cross. I was a bit wary of reaching my hands out for a spiritual life jacket. My hands where empty when I was homeless, so I reached out to the old, rugged cross. The cross of Jesus Christ keeps my soul afloat.

42

I was a lost ship in a stormy sea

I am amazed at the ship that are lost to the sea. The sea has claimed a lot of ships. The sea is so powerful. It is awesome in my own eyes. I watched its stillness, and I felt its power. I was like a lost ship at sea. I was caught in a storm of homelessness. I found no rest until the authorities caught me. I rest in prison let me know that I was not lost. A prison number lets you know that the authorities do not like you. I was found and I am no longer lost. The Apostle Paul was like a lost ship.

Jesus Christ found the Apostle Paul as he walked on the road to Damascus. The Apostle Paul spent a lot of time in the physical sea. The Apostle Paul was on a ship with two hundred men. The ship got lost in a storm. The Apostle Paul took bread, and he broke it. Not a life was lost on that ship. Do you feel like a lost ship in your personal life? It is easy to see that a homeless person is lost. A lot of homeless people are lost on the streets. The homeless people are looking for a material home.

I was the same when I was homeless. I also wanted to find a home for my weary soul. A person with a material home knows that his flesh is not lost. That same person knows that his soul could be homeless. Jesus Christ came to save the lost. A lot of his followers had material homes. Jesus Christ was not after saving their flesh. Jesus Christ was there to save their souls. I knew that my soul was homeless. My flesh was homeless and hungry. I drifted from place to place in my homelessness.

I want other people to be found. Life's will be changed when they find Jesus Christ. I have seen people finding Jesus Christ. It is such a delight to see their lives being changed. They become content with the simple things. The Holy Bible tells us that we are like lost sheep. The Holy Bible tells us that Jesus Christ is the good shepherd. The Holy Bible tells us that we are to enter the sheep pen. I want to change this to ships. Jesus Christ is like a harbour of amazing grace.

Jesus Christ is also called the light of the world. I see Jesus Christ as a light house. Is Jesus Christ calling you into a harbour of amazing grace. I have been pointing people to Jesus Christ for the last ten years. I have helped them to sail into the harbour of amazing grace. Do not go through your whole life being lost. Read about the good shepherd in the Holy Bible. That will show you my story. I am a sheep. I also like to call myself a ship.

Your flesh is not lost so you neglect the fact that your soul is lost. Look at a homeless person on the street. Put yourself in their position and you will feel scared. Imagine that your flesh is lost on the streets. I never had material a home in my homeless years. I grew up in a material home with a loving mother. That home was not a good place for a child. My drug infested council estate is full of lost souls. Does your soul feel lost? Seek Jesus Christ and ask him to sail you into a harbour of amazing grace. You will feel at home when you realize who Jesus Christ is. This short story is for the lost souls who are perishing in the red sea.

43

Saved by Jesus Christ in a storm

I lived in a stormy red sea. It was violent and dangerous for me. I was that young run away. Living through the storms weathered my life. I became tough and durable. I do shed a tear for the young boy who was lost in the storms. I created a lot of the storms. There are no more tears. Jesus Christ saved me from the storms. So many people are living in the storms of life. Do they know that Jesus Christ could save them? Every human has gone through a personal storm in their lives.

I was born and raised in the storms. Drug addiction is an escape from the storms. I do not boast about my old storms. A life of drugs and crime is not a life for young kids. Jesus

Christ saved me, and I am free. The storms still surround me, and I pray to the one who saved me. I do not live in the storms. I will be thrown back into the storms if I sin against my Lord. I was not an angel when Jesus Christ saved me from my storms. I tried to run back into my old storms.

My life became still, and I was used to the storms of my old life. Some people tried to drag me back into my old storms. I tried to drag them out of their storms. I am now aware of the dangers. There are dangers when you follow Jesus Christ into a calm sea. Jesus Christ is hope for the young people today. So many young people are living in the storms. Jesus Christ is there to rescue the drowning souls. Do not let the storms of life wet your dry eyes.

Your tears would run red if you were thrown into my old storms. There are different storms in this life. Some people handle them well. Other people cannot handle the storms. Call out to Jesus Christ if you are stuck in a storm. Do not be afraid to call out to Jesus Christ. My flesh went through the physical storms. My body is ravaged. My soul went through the spiritual storms. Jesus Christ mended my broken soul. My flesh healed its scars. Jesus Christ healed my inner scars.

We must recognize the people who are trapped in the storms. Their lives look still on the surface. They appear to be happy on the outside. I know that their insides are crying out. Some people are happy to stay in the storms. They are used to feeling depressed. Are you going through a mental health storm? I went through a crazy time of mental health. I was being tossed around in a storm of depression. There is no shame when you admit that you are suffering.

A problem halved is a problem shared. I spent a year in a treatment centre. Intense therapy could not calm the mental storms in my head. Jesus Christ had to take me out of the storms. I always sit at the sea when I am writing my short stories. I am writing this one because I know that people are drowning in a storm of mental health. The world behind me is going a little crazy. You hear about suicides and self-harm. Oh Lord let them see that you are the one they need. I say the Lords name and people mock me. They would not mock me if they sat here with me. I find perfect peace when I sit by the sea.

44

Standing by the sea in spiritual poverty

I love to stand at the sea on a day like today. I can now remember how far I have sailed in amazing grace. Are you standing in spiritual poverty? Jesus Christ has spiritual riches for you. I used to stand at this sea in my homeless years. I was standing in spiritual poverty. I stood in physical poverty in my homelessness. I remember standing by myself. Looking at the stormy sea was a blessing for me. Watching the waves crashing in was frightening for me.

Jesus Christ must have seen me standing here in my

homeless years. I stood alone for years. I thought that the world was a rich place. I sat begging on the streets. People appeared to be rich. I got to know people in the real world. It opened my eyes. The materially rich people where just as spiritually poor as I was in my homeless years. I struggled to understand these people. We were all born spiritually poor. Jesus Christ was sent to make us spiritually rich. Would you stand at the sea and admit that you are spiritually poor?

I stood by the sea. I am now spiritually rich. I want the world to be spiritually rich. A rich young man stood before Jesus Christ. The man asked Jesus Christ a few questions about eternal life. Jesus Christ told the young man to give away all his material wealth. The rich young man walked away from Jesus Christ. The rich young man loved his material wealth. How did Jesus Christ recognize that the rich young man was spiritually poor? I stood before Jesus Christ in my poverty-stricken life.

I had no material wealth, so I never had to make that decision. I am incredibly lucky in that sense. A poverty-stricken blind man stood before Jesus Christ. Jesus Christ said what do you want me to do for you. The poor blind man said I want to see. Jesus Christ gave the poor blind man his sight. Jesus Christ was able to heal him. The blind man never asked for material wealth. I have heard people saying that Jesus Christ has blessed them. Jesus Christ was crucified on the cross.

They had stripped his flesh to the bone. Jesus Christ looked materially poor as he was hanging on the cross. People stood around the cross. Jesus Christ said it is finished.

The people walked away spiritually poor. The disciples of Jesus Christ were spiritually poor in an upper room. The disciples stood in the mist of physical and spiritual poverty. The Holy Spirit fell amongst them. The disciples became spiritually rich. The disciples spread their spiritual riches to the poor.

The poor fell at the feet of the disciples. The disciples laid their hands on the poor. The poor were filled with spiritual riches. The eyes of rich men cannot describe this spiritual wealth. I received the same spiritual riches as the disciples. I have shared my spiritual riches with the poor. The Holy Bible will explain all this to you in your spiritual poverty. Are you prepared to give up your material wealth for spiritual riches? I was materially poor so I cannot answer that question for you. I now stand by the sea with my spiritual wealth in my short stories.

45

I was trapped in a spiritual whirlpool by the sea

I have only ever seen a small whirlpool. I let my bath water run away. The bath water made a little whirlpool. My drug addiction was like a whirlpool. I was born into a whirlpool of violence. I could not escape a whirlpool of guilt and shame. I have seen this whirlpool in action. The whirlpool of guilt and shame has claimed all sorts of sinners. The rich and poor have been sucked into a whirlpool of guilt and shame. This whirlpool of guilt and shame does not let you go.

I was battered in my whirlpool. I was washed around in my own blood. I was set free from my whirlpool. Jesus Christ drew me out of my whirlpool. I was born into a whirlpool, so I survived it. I feel for the people who were not born into a whirlpool of violence. They were drawn into it as they grew up. I tell people that they are stuck in a whirlpool. I also show people how my life has changed. The Holy Spirit has a whirlpool of amazing grace. I was drawn into a whirlpool of amazing grace.

I did try and stay in my whirlpool of guilt and shame. I was used to being washed around in my own blood. I asked Jesus Christ to let me go back to my old whirlpool. Jesus Christ does not hold you a prisoner, so I found myself back in my old whirlpool. I soon ran back into a whirlpool of amazing grace. I was not cut out for that old life. The change in my life was under way. This whirlpool of amazing grace will restore you into the image of Jesus Christ.

A whirlpool of amazing grace is without danger. You are free from your fears and tears. I do not have enough ink to explain this new whirlpool of amazing grace. The whirlpool of guilt shame has lots of sinners in it. Sinners are being spun around in depression and fear. Your world is like a big whirlpool of guilt and shame. I look at the disciples in the upper room. The disciples were caught in a whirlpool of fear. The

Holy Spirit fell in the upper room. The disciples were then sucked into a whirlpool of amazing grace.

The disciples burst out into the streets. The disciples preached repentance. Thousands of souls were sucked into this new whirlpool. This whirlpool of amazing grace swept itself over the world. The whirlpool of amazing grace is still pulling sinners into its centre. Are you stuck in a whirlpool of guilt and shame? Come and stand close to the whirlpool of amazing grace. You will see that lives are being changed. My pen is in a whirlpool of wisdom. The promises of Jesus Christ are true today.

I am sitting at the sea. I am being whirled around in a whirlpool of amazing grace. There is a whirlpool of guilt and shame and it is behind me. The world is one big whirlpool of guilt and shame. I will enter that whirlpool when I finish this short story. I will not be drawn into the worlds guilt and shame. I go into the world's whirlpool. I drag the poor out of its guilt and shame. What whirlpool will you choose today. Drag yourself to the cross. Confess your selfish sins. You will be sucked into a whirlpool of amazing grace when you start to believe in Jesus Christ.

46

Dredging the mouth of a spiritual sea

I am watching a dredger by the sea. The dredger is clearing a pathway for the ships. I am going to dredge up a short story for you. Jesus Christ is like a dredger for my life. I am like a channel that is leading out of the sea. My channel got blocked by my wilful sins. I now fight to keep my channel clear. I am escaping all distraction with my pen and paper. I am going to dredge up some of my past life. I will dredge it up. I will see the face of Jesus Christ.

All my fears and tears will be spilled into the channel. I ask Jesus Christ to make me a channel of his peace. Why do I dredge up my past life? It can hold me back from seeing the face of Jesus Christ. Jesus Christ is standing on the harbours wall. I want to sail up a channel of peace. I was brought up in a drug infested council estate. Growing up blocked my channel. I was cut off from knowing Jesus Christ. I fought the good fight in my teenage years. That fight left my channel blocked. The cross of Jesus Christ is for the poor people.

The poor people cannot dredge up their past sins. I will dredge a channel of peace for the poor sinners. I stand firm and I dredge up my past sins. The ships cannot dock in a harbour if we stopped dredging the mouths of the sea. The ships would be left exposed to the stormy sea. The captain of a ship knows the sea in the same way that I know Jesus Christ. A captain of a ship calls his deck hands. The captain says prepare for docking the ship.

The captain knows that he needs to protect his ship from the storm. The captain knows that a dredger would have made a way. What would happen if the dredger never did its job? The captain and ship would be left exposed to the storm. Are you looking for a way to escape your stormy sea? I am trying to dredge a path for you. Jesus Christ is calling you into a harbour of amazing grace. You cannot enter a harbour of amazing grace. Your channel is block by your past sins. Dredge your past sins up to the Lord Jesus Christ.

Confess your sins and you will see the way. I am following Jesus Christ. I want to dock my ship in a harbour of amazing grace. What is blocking your channel. We all have a channel that is full of fears. Some parents dredge a channel of love for their children. The children grow up and their channels become blocked by sin. I believe that Jesus Christ is guiding me in my writing. I am free to see the face of Jesus Christ. The Holy Bible tells us what separates us from amazing grace.

Sin separates us from Jesus Christ. The cross made away for us to know Jesus Christ. I love to sit by the sea. I am pleased that I dredged up this short story. You must dredge up your past sins. This can be painful for some people. I am always dredging up my past sins. I do it by the sea. Do not spend your life being stuck in the red sea. Jesus Christ is calling you to enter a harbour of amazing grace. I have helped a lot of sinners to dredge up their past sins. I watched these sinners finding perfect peace in a harbour of amazing grace.

47

A spiritual harbour for the lost ships

I can get a good look at a ship when it is docked up in a harbour. The ship is tied down to the harbours wall. The ship is safe from the stormy sea. The captain and crew can rest easy. I look back on my old life. I had nowhere to dock my ship. I was exposed to the storms at sea. I weathered the storms at sea. I was looking for a harbour to rest my wary soul. I ran away from home. I was a broken teenager. I was looking for a harbour of safety.

I found my harbour of safety in Jesus Christ. Jesus Christ is a spiritual harbour for the lost ships. I tie myself to the teachings of Jesus Christ. A lot of people do not have a harbour of safety. They are like a ship. They are being tossed around in the red sea. People have harbours of material wealth and yet their souls are lost in the red sea. So many people are shipwrecked in sin. The red sea is the world to me. Come all ye faithful. The Lord Jesus Christ has a harbour of amazing grace for you.

Would a parent not love to find a harbour of amazing grace for their innocent children. The innocent children are going to grow up in the red sea. Life will batter the innocent children into shipwrecks. Would a child not like to see their lonely parents in a harbour of amazing grace. Loneliness will strike in their old age. I see so much from the sea. I will leave it up to you to decide if people need to find a harbour of amazing grace. Why do I write so brightly when I am resting by the sea?

I write my pleas to the lost ships at sea. The Apostle Paul never took shelter in a harbour of amazing grace. The Apostle Paul went into the red sea. The Apostle Paul was a bit like me. I go into the red sea with Jesus Christ as my guide. I tell people that they are ships in the eyes of Jesus Christ. Do you know that Jesus Christ has a harbour of amazing grace? Do you feel locked out of the harbour of amazing grace? I know people who cannot find the entrance to the harbour of amazing grace.

This book of short stories is showing them the way. I was searching for a harbour of amazing grace. I knew that Jesus Christ was calling me into a harbour of amazing grace. I was scared to follow Jesus Christ into a harbour of amazing grace. I had to dredge up my past sins. It was painful for me. I did it and you can do it. God has not turned his back on your world. God gave us Jesus Christ on the cross. Jesus Christ defeated the cross for our sake.

The Holy Bible tells us everything that we need to know about God. Heaven is like a harbour of amazing grace. The Holy Bible tells us that some people will be turned away from

God's harbour of amazing grace. The sinners who turn to Jesus Christ will enter in. I am just an uneducated man who was once a homeless teenager. I lived by the sea. I found the secrets of heaven in my deep sea. The red sea is the world. The world has harbours of wealth and status. Some people are content with resting in a harbour of material wealth. Come to the cross and confess your sins. You will then enter a harbour of God's amazing grace.

48

Finding a plant by the sea

I wished that I had a plant in my homeless years. The seafront was covered in grey concrete. The concrete walls were to stop the waves from hitting me in the night. I walked a mile or two along the seafront. I found the sand dunes along the sea front. The grass on the sand dunes brought a bit of colour to my dull life. I know that it takes a strong plant to survive by the sea. I was also tough and durable in my homeless years. My drug addiction weakened me in the night.

I still survived my time by the sea. I rested on a bench by the sea. Other people were tucked up in a warm double bed. Was I richer than the people who were tucked up in a warm double bed? I was cold at night. I was looking for a plant. I watched the sea when other people were tucked up in their warm beds. The perfect setting sun was the sight that I watched. I had no home, so I watched the sun disappearing over the horizon.

I did not have a plant, so I planted my sinful eyes on God's creation. People put their lights out before they snuggled into a warm double bed. I was in my delight as I lay under the moon. No man in the heavens or earth could put the moons light out. I was lying flat out on an old wooden bench. Thinking about a plant sent me into a light sleep. I would wake up to a sun that was rising over me. Other people were crawling out of their commutable double beds. I would stretch my legs.

I then remembered my dreams. I dreamed that I would watch a plant flowing in the morning sun. The tide was rolling in. Other people were rolling into a busy day. I rolled my track suit bottoms up to my knees. I kicked of my trainers because I had to air my smelly feet. I walked along in the waves of the sea. There was no plant along the waves of the sea. I now see myself as a beautiful plant. My loving God planted Jesus Christ into my heart. I now blossom like the plant that I dreamed of.

I grow in the teachings of Jesus Christ. My roots soak up the teachings of Jesus Christ. I do not wake up homeless today. I do not have to kick of my trainers to air my feet. I rise out of my double bed in the mornings. I put my slippers on. I then water my house plants. The sea front always waits for me. I am now reflecting on my life by the sea. Do you feel like a dead plant by the sea? Jesus Christ will feed and water your roots if you believe.

Do you believe that my short stories are inspired by Jesus

Christ? The Holy Bible was written in the same way as these short stories. We must listen to the voice of Jesus Christ. I now plant my whole life in the teachings of Jesus Christ. I am now blossoming in this morning sunshine. Jesus Christ was preparing me to do a great work for him. I have helped people to blossom like my plant. You are a plant in the eyes of Jesus Christ. Read the teachings of Jesus Christ and you will blossom in his love. Put the teaching of Jesus Christ into practice and you will see God's love on an old, rugged cross.

49

Satan's freak waves striking me by the sea

The freak waves claim lives if they catch you out. You will only get wet if they do not wash you away. Freak waves were striking me in my young life. You start to except that you are being struck by freak waves. The freak waves strip you of your self-worth. You become worthless in your drug addiction. I stood against the freak waves of violence. I caused a lot of the freak waves in my young life. I used to say bring on whatever you have.

I watched people after Jesus Christ rescued me from the freak waves. People's lives appeared to be perfect. I then seen them being struck by a freak wave. One lady told me that

110

she had a commutable lifestyle. Her husband developed an illness. The husband had to give up his job. The money dried up fast. I listened to the lady's story. She told me that she used to look down on the poor people. I was in a midweek service at a church when she told me her story. I said that I loved to learn about Jesus Christ in a midweek service.

The lady told me the songs gave her mood a lift. Her commutable lifestyle was snatched away by a freak wave. This lady had many years of material wealth. I cannot share all her story in my short story. Her story was a sad one. I could tell you a thousand stories about people being struck by freak waves. I am happy that I survived the freak waves of violence. I was struck by many freak waves in my homeless years. I no longer hear freak waves of horrible words.

I would be begging on the streets. A freak wave of abuse would ring in my ears. Someone calling you a homeless scumbag is a freak wave of abuse. I heard it all from above. I sat on the dirty streets and I looked to the sky. Did Jesus Christ see me when I was getting verbal abuse for being homeless on the streets. I was unloved on the streets. I was often dripping in blood. I was struck many times. I never fell over onto the dirty ground. Other people are not so smart. Some people never rested at my resting place.

I watched the freak waves striking in the sea at night. Why do so many people get struck by freak waves? People are blind. They do not see the freak waves. I was struck by a nasty freak wave when I was barely twenty-one. My mother died. My grief stripped my flesh to my bones. I spend my twenties running into all sorts of freak waves. I was stripped inside out by that one freak wave. I was self-harming myself in a physical way. I had to tell you about my old freak waves.

The Holy Spirit struck my life like a freak wave. Everything was turned upside down by that moment in my life. A freak wave of the Holy Spirits grace does not claim your life. A freak wave of the Holy Spirits grace changes your life. Do you feel like you are being struck by negative freak waves? I have felt your pain. Ask my Jesus Christ to strike you with a freak wave of his amazing grace. A freak wave of amazing grace is going to wash itself over this sinful land. It will happen if people repent of their sins. A freak wave of the Holy Spirits grace washed over the streets of Jerusalem.

50
Digging a hole in the sand with a child's spade

I remember the day when I tried to dig a hole in the sand. I had found a child's spade on the sandy beach. I was homeless. I had time to spare on a hot summer's day. Thinking was my thing by the sea. I thought about things before I dug a hole in the sand. My drug addiction was not mine, but it had dug a hole into my life. Digging a hole in the sand was hard. My life was also hard. How deep can you dig in the dry sand before you hit the wet sand.

It is not that far if you are digging with a child's spade. I thought that my drug addiction would kill me. I thought that they would dig me a grave in the sand. That is not how my life was going to end. Jesus Christ stopped them digging me a grave in the sand. Jesus Christ pulled me out of a whole lot of trouble. I did not think that Jesus Christ could love me. I had dug myself to many sins for Jesus Christ to love me. I know that Jesus Christ loves me. They crucified Jesus Christ for my sins. Some people look like dry sand on the surface.

Did a little deeper into their lives. You will find that they are like the wet sand. I knew that my sins were keeping me in a hole of spiritual poverty. I never expected to dig into the teachings of Jesus Christ. I started to dig deeper, and I found water of another kind. Living waters is what I found. This living water started to quench my thirsty soul. I am sitting at the same spot where I dug a hole in the sand. I remember sitting with a child's spade in my hand.

Remembering my cheeky grin can bring a tear to my older eyes. The years have moved on. I remember this spot like it was yesterday. I am now digging up a short story for you. I know this sandy beach better than anyone. I lived here in my teenage years. I was stuck in a hole. The world looked down on me. I tried to climb out of my drug addiction on my own strength. My drug addiction had me trapped in a hole in the sand. I tried to climb out. The sides just fell in on me. Jesus Christ reached his pierced hands down to me.

I now look at people. They love to dig holes in their souls. They are trying to fill the hole in their souls with maternal wealth. The hole in your soul will only get bigger. Are you digging a hole in your soul? Does your worldly wealth satisfy the hole in your soul? I had no material wealth in my homeless years. I filled the hole in my soul with the love of Jesus Christ. You can dig into the teachings of Jesus Christ. I am always digging deeper into the teachings of Jesus Christ.

Do you appear to be dry sand on the surface? Dig up your past sins. You will see that you are like the wet sand. I did a study with a child's spade. This is what Jesus Christ has laid on my heart. I look at the homeless people. The homeless people are stuck in a hole of spiritual poverty. Jesus Christ wants me to pull the homeless people towards his amazing grace. I have dug up this short story out of nowhere. I will sit here for a while. I will remember the cheeky teenager who had a child's spade in his hands.

51

A tsunami of fear washing over this sinful land

We have all seen the damage that a tsunami can do if it washes over our sinful land. I want to tell you about another tsunami. The tsunami washed itself over my streets. A tsunami of heroin abuse washed itself over this land. A lot of innocent children got washed up in heroin abuse. I got caught up in the heroin tsunami. I grew up around drugs and crime. The tsunami of heroin abuse did not have any rules. The tsunami of heroin abuse had no mercy. I got hooked on the heroin.

Every two-bob bit nobody had a go at me. No place was safe for me. I was washed in a tsunami of red blood. My birth father was addicted to drugs. My birth father was always missing in my young life. I ended up taking drugs with my birth father. I was living in a drug den with my birth father. I woke up one morning and he was gone. My birth father popped in and out of my life for years. I found myself on my own again. A tsunami of violence threatened to kill me. Everyone turned on me.

I had robbed to many people. I had no protection from my family. I robbed them as well. My family had a big name. They never sheltered me. My mother stood by my side. My mother was fighting some of my battles. I do not glorify that old life. I was just a young kid who went off the rails. My family's name is something that I could claim. I am not one for fame so my family can keep their name. I am a child of Jesus Christ. I claim that Jesus Christ saved me from a family of criminals.

My uncle the powder king only brought shame on my family's name. The coward slandered my family's name by selling heroin to innocent children. My uncle was like a king to me when I was growing up. He turned on me when I robbed him. My Jesus Christ is a king in my life today. I bow down in wonder at his majesty. The cowards tried to bring me to my knees. I stood my ground in my teenage years. I now stand my ground in the teachings of Jesus Christ.

I wrote about a tsunami of heroin abuse. Let me tell you about a spiritual tsunami. The disciples of Jesus Christ were hiding away in an upper room. Jesus Christ delivered the promise of the Holy Spirit. The disciples burst into the streets of Jerusalem. The dispel Peter opened his mouth. A tsunami of words fell from his lips. A tsunami of amazing grace washed through the streets of Jerusalem. A real tsunami stops when the waves lose their power. The Holy Spirit never lost its power.

The Holy Spirit is still washing itself over this barren dry land. I was caught up in a tsunami of amazing grace. I do not want to get too excited about a spiritual tsunami. I believe that Jesus Christ could wash his forgiveness over this dry sinful land. A revival is just a tsunami of God's amazing grace. People fell on their knees when they were caught up in a spiritual tsunami. Communities were changed in the name of Jesus Christ. I pray that Jesus Christ will wash over this sinful land with a tsunami his father's forgiveness.

52
Looking at an iceberg in the sea

I remember watching a program about icebergs. I am now reflecting about this by the sea. One part of the iceberg was popping out of the sea. I could not see the hidden part of the iceberg. The bottom part of the iceberg was hidden under the waves of the sea. Oh Lord take me deeper into the heart of your sea. God was like an iceberg to my eyes. I could only see the tip of God's love on the cross. We were born spiritually blind to who God is.

I found the faith to explore below the waves of the sea. The bottom part of the iceberg is a hundred times bigger than the tip. Jesus Christ gave us the Holy Spirit. The Holy Spirit can open your spiritual eyes to the whole iceberg. Some people are happy to only see the tip of the iceberg. Open your blind eyes and Jesus Christ will reveal all his father's grace. The prophets seen so much of God's grace. It is written in the Holy Bible. God revealed himself to the prophets. The prophets looked at the whole iceberg.

Isaiah seen below the waves of the sea. Isaiah foretold the world that Jesus Christ would be heavens royal son. The writer of revelations told the world that Jesus Christ would return. The Holy Bible was written down by humble men. The humble men searched the sea. They prophets saw the whole iceberg. Why do I write about icebergs? I am just a humble man who was once a homeless teenager. I was brought up in a drug infested council estate.

I life of crime and prison brought me lost time. Jesus Christ struck me in the night. Jesus Christ told me to look below the waves of the sea. Oh lord is this the short story that you want me to explore. It easy to focus on the tip of the iceberg when you are full of selfish pride. It is hard to explore below the waves of the sea when you know the truth about Jesus Christ. I am in awe of what I write by the sea. I am not looking at the tip of the iceberg. I am looking deeper into the love that God had for his only begotten son.

I did a study with ice cubes in a class of water. I looked at the tip of the ice cubes. I then prayed to Jesus Christ. I said show me the part of the ice cubes that are under water. You can do this study when you have a class of water with ice cubes. See how much you are missing when you focus on the tip of the ice cubes. I am just so hot at writing a short story for Jesus Christ. My writing could melt the ice cubes in a glass of water. Look at God as if he was an iceberg.

You will see that his only begotten son is the tip of his love. Jesus Christ is asking you to explore his father's grace. There is more of God's love. God's love is trapped under the sea. Ask Jesus Christ to open your spiritual eyes to the whole iceberg. You will discover a God that loves you more than his only begotten son. I had to suffer much to see below the waves of the sea. I am pleased with my short story about icebergs. Jesus Christ does not surprise me anymore. Jesus Christ reveals himself when you search for the hidden part of the iceberg. I pray that you will find the hidden parts of God's amazing grace.

53
A horse walking along in the waves of the sea

This is a sight that I love to watch. A horse is walking along in the waves of the sea. I used to walk along in the waves of the sea. I was like this beautiful horse. This horse has a weight on its back. I also carried a weight on my back. I would love to see a horse without a weight on its back. This horse has a lady sitting on its back. I had a saddle of guilt and shame on my back. I can now see the weight that I was carrying. Jesus Christ lifted my weight with his pierced hands.

I was set free from my guilt and shame. I can now run along in the waves of the sea. I can kick out at the waves because my savour set me free. My life would have ended short if I had carried on walking with my guilt and shame. I lived a dangerous life by the sea. There is no danger when you walk in the footsteps of Jesus Christ. I do not commit crime, so I do not fear the police. This horse looks like it is free. The horse is not free when it has a saddle and reins on it.

I am free when Jesus Christ guides me in my short stories. I do not have reins on me. Jesus Christ does control the weight on my back. Jesus Christ called out to the people of Jerusalem. Come to me and I will lift your burden of weight. Do you feel like you are carrying a saddle of weight? Jesus Christ can lift your guilt and shame. Does this horse return to a field of weeds? Jesus Christ said that he has a field of lush green grass for you.

Draw back to Jesus Christ now and you will feed on his timeless teachings. This horse will get washed down after its walk in the sea. You could be washed in living waters if you believe. My dream is to own a horse. I will set my horse free by the sea. I will not let my horse carry a saddle on its back. My horse will run freely in the waves of the sea. I will follow my horse along the waves. I will kick out at the waves of the sea. I will fall over into the waves and Jesus Christ will catch me. Are you free to kick out at the waves of the sea?

This world has put a saddle on your back. You are weighed down with your selfish sins. The world has put reins on you. The world is leading you away from amazing grace. I am sitting in amazing grace today. I do not carry the weight of the world on my shoulders. I do not follow the world. Jesus Christ cut the reins of slavery for me. I look back to my teenage years. I can see the young boy who walked along in the waves of the sea. I know that Jesus Christ was looking down on me.

I am now free. I just want to praise my Jesus Christ. I pray that you will be set free. I pray that Jesus Christ will lift your saddle of guilt and shame. I pray that Jesus Christ will cut the reins that hold you to slavery. Jesus Christ came to set us free. I am free so I will write freely about Jesus Christ. I am pleased that I got to see a horse walking along in the waves of the sea. Jesus Christ is telling you that you are carrying a saddle of guilt and shame. Jesus Christ is telling you that the reins of slavery will hold you a prisoner. I pray that Jesus Christ will set you free.

54

The currents under the waves of the sea

I think about the currents that are hiding under the waves of the sea. I was being dragged around by the currents of fear. I tried to swim free from my drug addiction. It was all too powerful for me. I could not see that I was living in fear. My life dragged me in every direction. My guilt and shame pulled my life apart. I was dragged up in a drug infested council estate. I felt the pain of living in a drug infested council estate. I look at the surface of someone's life.

Their life looks calm to my human eyes. I know that the currents of fear are dragging them around. Everyone could see the currents of fear in my life. I was dragged around in a sea of my own blood. I felt the numbness in my face as a got struck. My lungs were emptied of air. My ribs cracked at the impact of a baseball bat. That was the physical currents in my old life. The physical currents left emotional currents under the surface of my life. I have good news today. I was pulled out of the currents of fear.

The currents of fear were going to drag me to my grave. I was scared when Jesus Christ started to pull me towards the cross. I was used to being dragged around in currents of fear. Jesus Christ had a battle on his hands with me. Why would Jesus Christ stop the currents from dragging me to my grave. I look in the mirror. I see a bloody pant. I now see what Jesus Christ sees in me. Jesus Christ was not interested in my external body.

Jesus Christ was concerned about my emotional currents. How are you feeling on the inside of your flesh? Are you showing everyone that your life is calm? Jesus Christ sees behind a false smile. Jesus Christ knows that the under currents are pulling your life apart. I know people who are in that position. They tell me about the under currents because I have been there. The currents of God's love are pulling me deeper towards the cross. I stand on a cliff and I overlook a red see. I can see that people are being pulled apart.

I cry out to the drowning souls. Repentance will stop the currents from dragging you to your grave. I repented my sins and Jesus Christ dragged me up a cliffs face. My old currents are not to be boasted about. I was going to die in a sea of blood. Look at your family and friends. They look perfect on the surface. They do not tell you that the under currents are pulling their lives apart. People will tell me because I know what it is like. I struggled when I found Jesus Christ.

I had the currents of my old life on one side. I had the currents of God's love on the other side. I was being pulled back and forth. I could not make up my mind. The world of crime and prison offered me an early grave. The currents of God's love offered me a new life. I choose the cross over my old life. Jesus Christ has used me in a big way. I have been pulling people out of the currents of fear. I am now sharing my story for you. Will you let the currents of God's love drag you to an old, rugged cross? Repent before the currents of fear drag you to an early grave.

55

Picking a seashell up from a sandy beach

I was just walking along the sandy beach. I was looking at all the different shells. I spotted one that I liked. I picked it up. I asked Jesus Christ to give me a short story. I now realise that I did not have an outer shell. I was born into a violent drug infested council estate. I had no protection against the violence. I had to develop my own shell. I climbed into a shell of isolation. My shell was empty. No one got into my shell. A crab takes a shell to protect itself. My young life was crazy.

I went into drug abuse at a young age. I was battered in my drug addiction. I did not have protection from my family. Everyone wanted to smash my shell. I am not ashamed to say that Jesus Christ came into my shell. Jesus Christ said let me dwell with you my child. I invited Jesus Christ into my empty shell. The Holy Spirit has filled my shell with amazing grace. Jesus Christ has slowly grown my shell. I have grown in my ability to write about his love. I grow in my faith and my shell becomes attractive.

I know people who are living in empty shells. Your flesh is

just a shell for your broken soul. Children are living in shells of fear. The children are afraid to believe in Jesus Christ. I know people who grew up and their parents neglected their needs. The parents wanted a material lifestyle, and their kids are now empty shells. People are filling their shells with worldly things. The things of this world will leave you feeling empty. I just picked up a shell. I prayed aloud.

I then picked up my pen and paper. Do you feel like an empty shell? Invite Jesus Christ into your shell. Jesus Christ will fill your shell with his amazing grace. Do you live in a commutable shell? You better watch out because life can smash you up. I have seen people like this. They were materially commutable, and their selfish sins smashed their commutable lifestyle. I picked my shell up and I put it to my ear. I heard the sea from my shell. I am like a shell. I want you to hear the waves of amazing grace.

Some people are living alone in their shells. I was homeless and alone. I know that loneliness can kill your soul. I do not feel lonely because Jesus Christ dwells in my shell. It can be hard to trust in Jesus Christ. God knows that his people are empty. The tomb was empty after the crucifixion. God send Jesus Christ to fill us up. I am filled up today. My love for you is flowing out of my shell. Have a look at Jesus Christ before you invite him in. Do not listen to preachers or church leaders.

Listen to the voice of Jesus Christ as you read the gospels in the Holy Bible. Your trust can be found in the teachings of Jesus Christ. Jesus Christ will shine a light into your dark shell. You do not need to live alone. I trusted no man in my old life. I trust Jesus Christ more because I picked up this little shell. I have written this short story for you. My shell is full of wisdom. Find your trust and invite Jesus Christ into your life. Your body is just a shell. The Holy Spirit wants to dwell within your shell. The Holy Spirit dwells within my shell. I write my short stories from within my shell of amazing grace.

56

Jesus Christ is a lifeguard by the sea

I used to watch the lifeguards by the sea. I watched them as I sat on my favourite bench. I did wonder why the lifeguards could not rescue me. The lifeguards were watching for people drowning in the sea. I was drowning in a sea of guilt and shame. Why could the lifeguards not rescue me from my guilt and shame. Everyone ignores the teenagers who are homeless. I was the homeless teenager. People ignored me. I sat begging on the streets. The public shouted at me.

I lifeguard does not always spot a drowning person in the sea. The public normally shouts out to the lifeguards. The lifeguards then jump in the sea. The public never shouted for someone to rescue me. The public shouted at me for being a homeless beggar. I am now safe from drowning in a sea of guilt and shame. Jesus Christ lifted me up from my sea of guilt and shame. I have lived and worked in society for a few years. I now realise that the public are drowning in the red sea.

Some people like to look down on the poor. It makes them feel better about their own spiritual poverty. I have become a little lifeguard for Jesus Christ. Tell me about a drowning soul. I will jump into the red sea to rescue them. I am sitting at the sea today. I remember watching the lifeguards by the sea. We are all called to be lifeguards to the poor. Would you love to become a lifeguard for Jesus Christ? Do you need a lifeguard to rescue you out of the red sea?

The world is behind me today. I am looking out over the waves. I can hear the cries from the world. I am writing a short story so the cries can wait. I will go into the world. I will spot a drowning beggar. I may just well share this short story with him. People walk past a homeless beggar as if they do not need a lifeguard to save them. They are not drowning on the surface. They have been shopping all day. Their bags of material wealth will keep their flesh afloat.

One day they will find that their souls are drowning in some sort of pain. I know that Jesus Christ is my lifeguard. Jesus Christ heard my cries in my homeless years. The public ignored me, and Jesus Christ reached his hands out to me. Call out to Jesus Christ if you see someone drowning. You can call out to Jesus Christ if you are drowning. Everyone will feel like they are drowning. Jesus Christ is the only name that can rescue the lost. I am nearly finished my short story. I will go into the world.

I will look for a drowning soul. My soul is alive when I seek to rescue a drowning soul. I know what it is like to be drowning in homelessness. I spent a lot of years on the streets. I will never forget the people who are homeless today. I have been a lifeguard to a lot of people over the years. I rescue them and they thank me. I tell them not to thank me. I tell them that Jesus Christ sent me to be their lifeguard. Let Jesus Christ be your lifeguard. You will receive his father's forgiveness if you repent of your sins. Tell a homeless person that Jesus Christ loves them.

57

Holding a grain of sand in my hand

I am holding a handful of sand in my hand. I could not count the grains of sand in my hand. I can count the years when I was alone by the sea. I remember the days when I was locked up in a prison cell. I can now count the time that I have spent in the loving arms of Jesus Christ. The Holy Spirit can pick you out of a handful of sand. Jesus Christ can then set you free for a mission. Your society is my handful of sand. There are a lot of sinners in your society.

I tell people that I have been set apart to do a great work for Jesus Christ. Some of these people mock me for believing in Jesus Christ. I am special in my life. I let Jesus Christ set me apart. I was set apart from your society when I was homeless. I was set apart from society when I grew up in a drug infested council estate. I was never a part of society, so

Jesus Christ plucked me out from my homelessness. I know people who go to church. They tell me that they do not feel Jesus Christ in their hearts.

They are no different to the sinners in your society. To go to church is not enough to set you apart. You can praise Jesus Christ with songs of praise, and you will not feel him in your heart. I believed in Jesus Christ and he set me apart. I was set apart from the handful of sand. I was probably lucky because I was set apart in my homelessness. The love of Jesus Christ tells me that I am a special grain of sand. People have told me that they can see my love Jesus Christ.

Some people have said that they want to know Jesus Christ in their hearts. I take them to church. I pray with them. I tell them that they must set themselves apart from the world. I tell them that they must commit themselves to the service of Jesus Christ. They choose to be a part of the world. They will accept life's struggles because they live in the world. They are fine if they can find their next quick fix. A holiday or something new will satisfy that need in their hearts.

People chase the imitate gratification to material things. I will never let the world entice me with its worldly things. I was never a part of your society. I have now lived and worked in society for years. I still do not fit into your society's way of life. No one knows my past. People slag of the homeless to my face. No one knows that I was a scumbag in my drug addiction. People slag of the drug addicts to my face. How can I bond with these people?

I have a friend in Jesus Christ so I will never be a friend of your society. It breaks my heart when people slag of the poor.

I will conform to your society, but I will never be its slave. I am free when I sit by the sea. The Holy Bible tells us that God sets his people apart. These people became servants of our God. Jesus Christ is the one who set me apart. There was a man named Saul. Saul was walking on the road to Damascus. Jesus Christ blinded Saul. Saul was then set apart to serve Jesus Christ. This man Saul was renamed. Saul became the Apostle Paul. The Apostle Paul wrote a lot of the new testament. Have a look at the Apostle Paul in the Holy Bible. Would you let Jesus Christ set you apart?

58

Jesus Christ rescued me from a stormy sea

Oh lord how I love to sit by your sea. Oh Lord you came and rescued me just in time. My Lord pulled me out of my stormy sea. My Lord took my hands as the currents were pulling me to my grave. My Lords voice stilled my once violent sea. One word from my Lord and the sea obeyed. My Lord was mightier than my old shame and pain. I would have drowned in a sea of tears. I am now casting my net out in my writing. Are you caught in my old stormy sea?

My Lords love will pull you from your sea of pain. Jesus Christ threw me a lifeline. My hands reached out. Jesus

Christ then cradled this broken child. I fought against my Lords love for a long time. I was like a wild salmon, I swam away from God's grace. The mouth of the sea was blocked by my past sins. My Lord made away for me to make it home. I swam up a river of living waters. My Lord was the salt of God's earth. The salt of the earth was to preserve me for eternal life. All my salty sins were spilled out into a channel of love.

My Lord called fisher men from the sea. My Lord draws me back to the sea with a pen and paper. My Lord wants me to reveal his love to you. My Lord gave all his power to the moon. The moon draws the seas back and forth. My Lord made away for me to reveal my needs to the sea. I have no defence for loving Jesus Christ. I once stood on a sea defence. I asked my Lord to roll his waves over your barren dry land. Waves of living waters will quench the thirst in a baby's soul.

Is your soul to dry to call upon my Lord's name. I say my Lords name and people look ashamed. These people are hiding their guilty sins under a red sea. These people do not have a captain on their rafts of spiritual poverty. I will throw my Lords name to the ends of the earth. Are you on a raft without a paddle? I will paddle through this short story for you. I just write what I see in me. I am no longer caught in a stormy sea. The waves of guilt have settled like a baby in its mother's womb.

The currents of guilt no longer pull me away from the cross. I was pulled from the sea by a force that I could not see. I was scared until I heard his gentle voice. Are you free to write about your rescue? Are you still stuck in my old stormy sea? I was homeless by the sea. I know what power the sea holds below its waves. I have just taken a breath. My Jesus Christ can move this pen. What does it feel like when you are pulled out of the stormy sea? I cannot share to many of my feelings with you.

It was all a bit emotional for me. I tried to fit into the world behind me. That world hurt me when it rejected me. I crawled away from the sea. I made my way back into your world. Your world wants to see people drowning in the storms. Society tried to kick me back to the sea. Jesus Christ told me to fight for my place in your society. I have fought to stay in your society. I want to rescue the poor from the red sea. I am pleased with my short story. My Jesus Christ rescued me from a violent stormy sea.

59

Looking for a lifeboat in a stormy sea

A like to look at the lifeboats by the sea. Call for the lifeboat and they will come and rescue you from the sea. I was drowning in a sea of guilt and shame. I was looking for a lifeboat in my stormy sea. Jesus Christ pulled me aboard his lifeboat. Jesus Christ pulled me aboard as my society was judging me. Jesus Christ now calls me to point the sinners towards his lifeboat. I will point the poor sinners towards the lifeboat. I respect the lifeguards who go out in their lifeboats

These men and woman do not fear the stormy sea. Some of them have lost their lives to the sea. I could boast about my old stormy sea. I will only boast about Jesus Christ being a lifeboat. I know what it is like to drown in a sea of blood. It was meant to be a bloody drowning for me. A few people did try and murder me. I am sitting by the sea, so they failed to put me in a grave. Are you looking for a lifeboat to rescue you? I know that your flesh is not drowning in the physical sea.

I know that your soul could be drowning in a spiritual sea. I know what it is like to be rescued. Jesus Christ was sent to be a lifeboat to the poor. The poor people are looking for a lifeboat. It is my job to point them towards Jesus Christ. I always wanted to volunteer to be a lifeguard. I used to watch them practising out at sea. The lifeboats are powerful vessels. They are equipped with the latest safety gear. The lifeboats where not like that a hundred years ago.

I did a bit of research on the history of the lifeboats. I looked at the photos from a hundred years ago. You would have to of been mad to go out in the old lifeboats. The men and women were made of steal. Let us get back to Jesus Christ. Do you see Jesus Christ as a lifeboat? I see Jesus Christ as a lifeboat. I was pulled aboard by a force that I could not see. I can now see because I am not drowning in guilt or shame. I would love you to come aboard the lifeboat. We have a captain who cares for us.

I watched people getting pulled aboard the lifeboat. They

were so happy to know that Jesus Christ had rescued them. They never seemed to bother about the people who were still drowning. These people were selfish. They found them self's back in the stormy sea. I stay in the lifeboat because I am always dragging the poor sinners aboard the lifeboat. I tell them all about my Jesus Christ. The poor sinners are grateful. I will sit by this sea. I will look out for a lifeboat passing by.

I will think about the person who is drowning in the physical sea. I look over my shoulder. I can see a sinful world. Peoples souls are drowning on the dryland behind me. I will make my way home. I will spot a homeless person. I may sit a while with him. I will tell him about Jesus Christ being a spiritual lifeboat. That is what a believer is called to do. I find it easy because I once sat on the streets begging. I know what it is like when society looks down on you. I also know what it is like when Jesus Christ plucks you into a lifeboat of amazing grace. Come abord the lifeboat and you will be safe.

60
Finding a holy wind for my sails in a storm

I like to look at sailing boats by the sea. I am now thinking about where I was sailing to in my young life. I used to be sailing in drug addiction. I was like a lost sailing boat. I had no wind to propel me away from my drug addiction. Things changed for me one day. A man laid his hands on me. This man prayed that I would be filled with a holy wind. This holy wind sailed to change my lifestyle. I was afraid of change, so I pulled my sails in. I could not let go of my windless life.

I then realised that Jesus Christ loves me. I put my sails back up. I said Jesus Christ you blow my sails, and I will preach your name. I preached the good news. I started to change my life. I did not want to leave the seaside. Jesus Christ was sailing me into the real world. I sailed into a selfish society. Jesus Christ never changed my cheeky personality. My cheekiness got me into society. I was still me, but my drug addiction was gone. I got myself a flat and a job.

I will not share to much about my sailing the good news. I will let you know what Jesus Christ taught me. I could say that it was all joyful and that would be a lie. Letting go of my life by the sea was hard. Jesus Christ said that I could always visit the sea. I love a man by the name of Paul. Jesus Christ put a holy wind into Pauls sails. You can discover his story in the Holy Bible. Reading the Holy Bible generates a breeze in your soul.

Put the Holy Bible into practice and you will receive a hurricane wind in your soul. This hurricane wind can tear your sails. Study the Holy Bible before you put it into practice. Jesus Christ put me in the real world. I started to notice that people are windless. They do not have a holy wind in their souls. I cannot believe that these people judged me in my homeless years. These people are trying to generate a wind through material wealth. I know believers who are in a windless place. They do not pick up their Holy Bibles.

They are not brave enough to put the Holy Bible into action. Faith without action will leave your soul in a windless place. My Jesus Christ is blowing my ink onto my paper. The sails on my pen are moving me along. Let us look at Pentecost. The disciples are hiding in an upper room. Jesus Christ has left them alone. The disciples wait on the promise. Jesus Christ told the disciples that he would deliver a promise. There was a mighty rushing wind. The holy wind swept itself through the upper room.

The disciple's souls where being blown by this holy wind. The disciples sailed into the streets of Jerusalem. I received the same holy wind as the disciples. I have sailed through the last ten years in amazing grace. Is your soul in a windless place. Would you love to be swept along in amazing grace? A disciple approached a lame beggar. The disciple said arise in the name of Jesus Christ. The lame beggar stood up. The beggar was healed, and he danced to the temple. The lame man's soul was filled with a holy wind. I was just a homeless teenager. I found Jesus Christ and I danced to the sound of amazing grace. I pray that you will find this holy wind in your windless life.

61

Standing in front of the sea in spiritual poverty

I stood in front of the sea for years. I was so free in my homeless years. I ran to the sea. That is as far as I could run. I could not run away from my past. I put my back to the sea. I then looked at the world. I did not belong in the world. I was surrounded by violence when I grew up. My drug addiction caused me a little bit of trouble. I was always looking over my shoulder. I had to fight for my life a few times. I was set up by the people I should have trusted. I have been trapped in houses.

I could write about the danger in my old life. I stood in front of the sea. I then heard a song for the first time. I found the meaning to my life in a song. The song says that Jesus Christ split the sea in two. Jesus Christ never splits the physical sea. Jesus Christ split a spiritual sea for me. I love the sea. The song has more meaning to my life. My physical body healed itself naturally. My soul could not heal itself on its own. I needed Jesus Christ to mend my broken soul. I stood at the sea for years.

My ears were closed to that beautiful song. Jesus Christ was asking me to walk through an open sea. The Holy Bible has an attachment to the sea. The Holy Bible seems to relate itself around the sea. A lot of people come to the sea. People look at the waves and then they are on their way. I stood at the sea for years. I cried out at the roaring waves for years. Me and the sea are attached. I love to think by the sea. I stand here writing a short story. Sometimes I do not want to write about my life.

I just stand here, and I wonder why Jesus Christ loved me. Why could he not just let me be with the sea. I have a concrete world behind me. The concrete world has more problems than me. The concrete world gives me sore feet. I stand here and I remember when I walked on the sandy beach. I slept under the moon and stars. I sometimes stand here, and I am torn in two. I have had enough of living in your concrete world. I have been living in the concrete world for ten years.

My daughter is now twenty-seven years old. She came to live with me when she was barley a teenager. I gave her a life that no other teenager had. I got my teenage years back through my daughter. I now have a grandchild and I am so young. I have taught my daughter about the sea. My daughter said dad I cannot wait until you teach your grandchild about the sea. My grandchild is only a few months old. I stand here and I am praying to Jesus Christ.

Oh lord give me the strength and wisdom to teach my grandchild about the sea. I fear for my grandchild in your concrete world. I sometimes call world the red sea. I took my grandchild to church at Christmas. Do you see my point of standing at the sea? I am standing here. I am asking Jesus Christ why he has given me this responsibility. A grandchild is for life and not just for Christmas is his reply. I am going to struggle to bring a grandchild up in a concrete world. The Lord will remind me of my old life on another day. I am going to stand here for a while with Jesus Christ.

62
Smashing into the breakwater rocks in a storm

I stand on these breakwater rocks. It is another day. I can imagine myself getting washed into these rocks. I was smashed against the rocks in my old life. A baseball bat is like a rock. My ribs cracked at the impact of a bat. The sharp rocks are like the knifes that tried to slash me apart. I bled a lot. My blood turned me into a rock-solid teenager. This rock-solid man should hate the people who smashed me into the rocks. I am capable enough to smash them into the rocks.

I was solid enough to stand against the violence. I have decided that I am not capable of revenge. Jesus Christ is now the rock that I love to stand on. I stand firm in the promise of forgiveness. Jesus Christ said that he would send us a helper. A helper could help me to forgive the cowards and bullies. I remember asking Jesus Christ to save me. I was being smashed into the breakwater rocks. Jesus Christ said stand on my teachings. The teachings of Jesus Christ are like a big solid rock.

All the other ground is sinking sand. People are sinking in unforgiveness. There is power in the name of Jesus Christ. Jesus Christ looked down from the cross. Jesus Christ seen the people who had crucified him. Jesus Christ said father forgive them for they do not know what they are doing. I could not hurt the bullies and cowards. People who forgive little receive little. People who forgive much receive much more. Do you feel like someone has smashed you into the breakwater rocks?

Could you stand at the sea and forgive them? My uncle was a hard man to some people. I see him for what he is. Someone told me that my uncle is now a broken man. This uncle offered me no protection. I must pray for his salvation. He is now getting smashed into the breakwater rocks. I live in your society. People are getting smashed in the breakwater rocks. I was physically smashed up. The blood pouring from my face told me that it was physical.

Jesus Christ is telling me about our emotional wellbeing. You could be emotionally damaged in your life. Everything looks ok on the surface. You are not suffering blood loss like I did. The breakwater rocks left me an emotional wreck. Jesus Christ restored my mind to some sort of normality. There is nothing normal about me living in your society. The Holy Bible teaches us that we are broken. Your concrete world has breakwater rocks in it. An abusive relationship is a sharp rock.

The loss of a loved one is a double-edged sharp rock. I know that Jesus Christ sees your pain. The currents of lust will pull you towards the breakwater rocks. Your selfish sins will smash you against the breakwater rocks. Jesus Christ can pull you away from the breakwater rocks. It takes a lot of faith to believe in my story. It does not take faith to believe that my short stories are inspired by Jesus Christ. Watch out for the breakwater rocks. I am finished for the day. Are your sins smashing you into the breakwater rocks? Repent of your sins and Jesus Christ will save you from your sorrows.

63

Shifting sand blowing along a sandy beach

I was always shifting around in my young life. I could not find a place to settle down. I ended up settling down on a sandy beach. I look at the sand. I feel how light the sand is. I am reminded how light I was on my feet. I was not like a grain of sand in the wind. I was to get the wind knocked out of my sails. The wind will take a dry grain of sand along the sandy beach. I was a wet grain of sand. The wind would not move me along the sandy beach.

I am now a dry grain of sand in the eyes of Jesus Christ. The Holy Spirit has blown me on to a sand dune. I look at the houses from this sand dune. The sand has blown itself around the houses. The people cannot move the sand back onto the sandy beach. The sand has been contaminated when it lands in their gardens. Some people are like the contaminated sand. Their sins have left them feeling contaminated. I am sitting on a sand dune with Jesus Christ. I tell people that they are welcome to join us.

People will not join us on the sand dune. People feel contaminated by sin. People do not want to confess their selfish sins. I want you to believe in shifting sand. Jesus Christ wants to blow you towards a sand dune of forgiveness. It is time to shift yourself into a good position. I am praying for a holy wind. This holy wind will turn you into a dry grain of sand. Jesus Christ will then blow you onto a sand dune. The grasses on the sand dune will hold you in amazing grace.

I am sitting on a sand dune of amazing grace. I was a contaminated grain of sand. I told Jesus Christ that I was a dirty grain of sand. I told Jesus Christ that I was a wet grain of sand. I confessed my sins. I then became a dry grain of sand. Jesus Christ blew me onto a sand dune of forgiveness. I was born into a drug infested council estate. I was told that I could not leave my estate. It was all wet stuff. I was left dripping in blood. I ran away from my drug infested council estate. I found myself sitting on a sandy beach.

No one wanted me to escape my drug infested council estate. My drug infested council estate is like a sand dune of hate. You become a part of the sand dune of hate. People try and leave the sand dune of hate. Society traps you on the sand dune of hate. You try and leave the sand dune of hate and they throw you into a prison. I shifted around the prisons in my teenage years. I was treated like that in my drug infested council estate. This boy escaped the sand dune of hate. I ran away from it.

I ended up sitting on a sandy beach. I found Jesus Christ and he placed me on a sand dune of amazing grace. You are welcome to join me on this sand dune of amazing grace. Do not let the world trap you on a sand dune of hate. Jesus Christ is calling you onto a sand dune of amazing grace. Dry your eyes and Jesus Christ will blow you on to a sand dune of amazing grace. I am sitting here on a sand dune of amazing grace. I feel special today. I sit here with my pen and paper. This is the short story that was laid on my heart for you.

64

Picking seaweed up from a sandy beach

I walk along the beach. I pick up some seaweed. I was like this pile of seaweed in my homeless years. I stank of spiritual poverty. No one wanted to pick me up when I was homeless. I took the drugs to block my sense of smell. I was blind to the neglect that I was putting myself through. I look at the seaweed that has been washed up on the beach. I look to the sky. I remember getting washed clean. Jesus Christ stooped down to wash his disciple's feet. Jesus Christ took the smell of my seaweed.

My seaweed was my guilt and shame. Do you feel like you stink of seaweed? What fragrance did the lady pour over the head of Jesus Christ. The fragrance of amazing grace can speak of God's love. Some people believe that they deserve to stink of guilt and shame. A homeless beggar looks smelly on the outside. Do you know that a homeless beggar has a soul? His soul could smell as bad as his outward appearance. I was a homeless beggar. My soul stank of guilt and shame.

I sat by the sea and Jesus Christ washed my soul clean. I could not believe that normal people could stink as bad as me. I started to live in society. I noticed something strange. Normal people do stink on the inside. Their outward appearance disguises the smell of guilt and shame. These are the people who look down on the smelly beggars. I have heard it all in society. I took a smell of my society. I then ran back to the sea. The smell of bitterness and envy is all around your society.

I must escape the smell of bitterness, so I find myself by the sea. Your friends and family will tell you how sweet you smell. You know the smell of your own selfishness. The smell of sin separates you from Jesus Christ. Repent your sins and you will start to smell of amazing grace. Why do people look down on the homeless people? A homeless person's appearance can be deceiving. I was homeless. I lived with other homeless people.

A homeless person's compassion would leave you smelling of jealousy. I must fight hard to keep the smell of amazing grace in my soul. Living in society can make me judgemental. I should not judge the people who judged me in my homeless years. They are just as smelly as a homeless person's feet. What is the point of this story? Jesus Christ knows that we smell of guilt and shame. Jesus Christ wants to spray your soul in amazing grace. Do not be ashamed if your soul stinks of bitterness.

There are a thousand things that make you smell of seaweed. There is one name that makes you smell of amazing grace. I love the fact that a lady poured a jar of perfume over the head of Jesus Christ. I am humbled by the fact that Jesus Christ stooped down to wash his disciple's feet. My feet stank in my homeless years. I woke up in the morning. I kicked of my trainers. I pulled a pair of dirty socks of my feet. I then walked in the waves of the sea. I was set free from the smell of my feet. You could be set free from the smell of guilt and shame if you believe in Jesus Christ.

65
The salt from the sea eroding a house away

Why is the sea so salty? I once swam in the sea. It was a red-hot summers day. The sea would be more pleasant if it lost its salty taste. I look at the houses on the sea front. These people can afford to keep them looking nice. I walk away from the sea front and I spot some other houses. The houses are just of the sea front. Some of the houses are looking distressed. The sea water is being blown onto the houses. The salt from the sea is eroding the houses exterior away.

I think about my old life by the sea. My sins were like the salt from the sea. My sins were eroding my soul away. People walk past me today. I look like a well-kept house. I was like an eroded house when I was homeless by the sea. We are all like the sea. We hide our sins like the sea hides its saltiness. Your sins are rotting your soul away. We try to cover the damage in our souls with our outward appearance. My drug addiction was like the salt from the sea.

I was eroded inside out by my drug addiction. No one wanted to talk to me when I was homeless by the sea. Jesus Christ loves the people who are eroded away by sin. Does your outward appearance resemble the pretty houses overlooking the sea? Does your soul resemble an old, eroded house away from the sea front? We taste the salt in the sea. The salt leaves a bitter taste in our mouths. Your sins leave a bitter taste in God's mouth. I watched an old, eroded house by the sea.

The old, eroded house was for sale. Someone bought that house and they restored it. I watched the progress over a few months. They ripped the windows out and they took the roof off. I watched them ripping the plaster from the outside walls. They put in new windows and a roof. They replastered the outside and they painted it white. My soul was like an eroded house and Jesus Christ did that to me. I am now like a perfect house by the sea. I sit here with my pen and paper.

I remember how much Jesus Christ loved me. Does your soul feel like an old, eroded house by the sea? Let Jesus Christ rip your life apart. You will become the beautiful house that Jesus Christ intended you to be. I am not materially rich in my life. I am spiritually rich in my life. The people who own the pretty houses by the sea could be rotting away on the inside. We can hide our sins like the sea hides its saltiness. You cannot hide your sins from the eyes of God.

God sent his only begotten son to restore us. You will be restored in perfect grace when you believe. Do not judge a homeless person who is eroded away on the outside. I was that homeless person. I was eroded inside out. Jesus Christ restored me inside and out. I love to see a lost soul being restored in perfect grace. We should be helping to restore a homeless person's self-worth. Everyone is struggling with their self-worth. Some people hide it by their outward appearance. Would you let Jesus Christ restore you? You are a house in the eyes of God. Your house could become a dwelling place for the Holy Spirit.

66
Dreaming about living on a fishing boat

I used to watch the fishing boats when I was homeless. I stood at the waves of the sea. That is as far as I could run. I dreamed of living on a fishing boat. I could not escape this island, so I looked at fishing boats. I thought about casting my nets far and wide. I used to wonder how wide the sea was.

I knew that I was very wide in my teenage years. My life was like a fishing boat in a storm. I lived a dangerous life. The fishing boats are left at the mercy of the sea.

I was left at the mercy of my drug addiction. A storm will claim the biggest of fishing boats. The remains of fishing boats are lying at the bottom of the sea. Jesus Christ was teaching by the Sea of Galilee. The crowds were pushing towards Jesus Christ. Everyone wanted to hear the voice of Jesus Christ. Jesus Christ called for a man's fishing boat. Jesus Christ entered the boat and he spoke to the crowds. You can read his parables in the Holy Bible. Why did Jesus Christ call some disciples away from their fishing boats?

These humble men had careers in the fishing industry. They must have seen something in the eyes of Jesus Christ. Jesus Christ said follow me and I will make you a fisher of men. We can look back and see how the story unfolded. These fishermen became history makers. Did they know that Jesus Christ would lead them to the cross? I never got to live on a fishing boat. I was penniless when Jesus Christ called me away from the sea. I had no job or prospects.

I had nothing to offer Jesus Christ in my life. I know that Jesus Christ wanted me to be a fisher of men. I have done a good job of that. Jesus Christ is even asking me to lay my life bare on a bit of paper. I still dream of living on a fishing boat. Jesus Christ will not give me that wish. Jesus Christ knows that I struggle to live your society. I have been trying to escape this selfish island for years. You can run away from society, but you will hit the sea water. I will just have to settle for looking at fishing boats.

I can imagine the freedom of living on a fishing boat. Jesus Christ travelled over the Sea of Galilee in a fishing boat. Jesus Christ was sleeping in the hull of a fishing boat. A storm swelled up from the east. The disciples cried out for Jesus Christ to save them. I believe that Jesus Christ stayed on a fishing boat. Everyone was looking for him. Jesus Christ was healing the sick, so people were looking for him. I know that Jesus Christ would have rested on a fishing boat for a night or two.

I wish people could see that Jesus Christ lived by the Sea of Galilee. It was a different life two thousand years ago. The disciples would have loved their jobs. The disciples were coming ashore in a fishing boat. Jesus Christ called out from the shoreline. A disciple noticed that it was Jesus Christ and he dived into the sea. The disciple got to dive from his fishing boat. I am just sitting here with a dream. I am finished with this short story. I will sit here, and I will watch the fishing boats. You can read about the disciples and their fishing boats in the Holy Bible.

67

Swimming in the sea on a hot summer's day

I was homeless by the sea. I remember the day when I swam in the sea. It was a red-hot summers day. I would normally just walk in the waves, but this day was hot. I swam along in three foot of water. My arms tired. I then rolled on to my back. I kicked my feet, and I propelled myself along the waves. I investigated a clear blue sky. I want to tell you about another sea of water. Jesus Christ said that he has a sea of living waters. Is your soul thirsting for living waters.

The living waters will quench your thirsty soul. Have you ever read about Jesus Christ by a well? It is a great story. The story leads me to the sea of living waters. A hot summers day will have you thirsting for a cold glass of water. Jesus Christ asked the lady by the well for a drink of water. Jesus Christ new that the lady was spiritually thirsty. Why is my heading about swimming in the sea? I believe that all wells lead to streams. All streams lead to rivers. All rivers lead out into the sea.

So, there must be a sea of living waters. It is not hard to believe if you have received the first promise. Receive the Holy Spirit and everything will become believable. I was born dry. I was raised in a desert. My desert was a drug infested council estate. My soul is not dry, and my pen is not dry of ink. Are you clean enough to swim in a sea of living waters? Ask Jesus Christ to give you a drink from the well. Ask Jesus Christ to walk down the stream with you.

Ask Jesus Christ to guide you down the river. You will then find the sea of living waters. I had to be homeless by the sea. All this would be hard to believe if I spent my life in your concrete world. People are thirsting after lustful things. You could be swimming in a sea of money. The money will not satisfy that thirst in your soul. I have gotten to know some rich people. There is something spiritually poor about them. I would love them to see Jesus Christ for who he was. Young people will never know the truth about Jesus Christ.

Our children are being brought up in a materialistic world. I was brought up in physical poverty. I never tasted the high life in a material world. I am looking at the spot where I swam in the sea. It is so hard for me to believe who I am today. I did not know the Holy Bible when I swam in the sea. I now know that the Holy Bible is a mirror image of the sea. Why would God place his only begotten son by the Sea of Galilee? Jesus Christ was baptised in the river Jordon.

The river Jordan runs into a sea. I wish it were a red-hot summers day because I would go back in the sea. I would float on my back and I would remember a time when I was free. I cannot swim in the sea today. I must go back into your concrete world. I will look at people in society. I know that they are thirsting for living waters. Their material wealth is making them ill. I really hope that you will search for the sea of living waters. My story should give you clues to where it is. Research the Holy Bible for clues. Start your search with Jesus Christ by the well with a woman.

68

Starlings making music as they fly over the sea

Are the starlings making music in the sky? I sit on the sand and I pray. Birds in numbers are making a dance in the sky. I want to compose a melody for Jesus Christ. The starlings are twisting and turning in the sky. Shapes appear as they woosh away from me. Their wings are within touching distance. The timing is key for Gods' beautiful birds. Oh Lord give me the keys to heavens front door. I cannot picture something more in tune with each other than my thousand starlings.

The sunset is on the horizon. The starlings are dancing to God's sunset. They are brushing their wings within a whisper of each other. I brushed with death in my teenage years. I cannot fly with a thousand starlings. I tried to fly with my society. My society beat me down because I was on the drugs. Alone and homeless was my dance in my teenage years. No one wanted to brush against my dirty wings. I watched the starlings in the sky. The colours in the sky told me to open my spiritual eyes.

The sunset is starting to say its goodbyes. The background colours tell the starlings to roost under a pier in a seaside town. I sat under the pier with a thousand starlings. The birds settle as I walked into town. I find myself a doorway and I sit down. The town is packed with a thousand drunken revellers. I watch the hen party going from the pubs to the clubs. The hen party was trying to dance on the roads. The stag party looked down on me. I was cold and hungry.

My clothes never suited me in a doorway. I looked to the sky. I felt my tears running down my cheeks. I rubbed my eyes, and I felt my cheek bones. The tears in my eyes where not for the drunken dancers. My tears where for the thousand starlings in the sky. I did not need their loose change. I watched something that money cannot buy. I now see beauty in my ink. I am dancing with Jesus Christ on the sand. The Holy Spirit was described as a lone bird. The Holy Spirit danced out of the sky over the river Jordan.

A voice followed the dance. The voice said this is my only begotten son. The beauty of a thousand starlings could not overshadow the love that God had for his son. The cross was ahead of Jesus Christ. Jesus Christ danced to the cross for my sins. The cross was to show the thousand drunken revellers that they are loved. You only start to look for Jesus Christ when you are homeless and unloved. I am now a grown man. I am sitting by the sea. I am free to write with clear eyes.

I have a soft heart for Jesus Christ because I can see the cross. The whooshing of starling's wings is ringing in my ear. I am still a solo dancer. Your society still judges me. A lone starling cannot pull of a dance, but a lone teenager can write a poem of love. Jesus Christ calls us to be like the starlings. We should be brushing our wings together. The Holy Spirit could bring us within a whisper of each other.

We could make a dance on this very earth. The dance that I described in my short story was played out at Pentecost.

69

Sitting on a sandy beach looking at beach huts

What would I have given for a beach hut in my homeless years? WitchWhich colour would I of painted my beach hut. A nice blue colour would have suited me. I remember walking past the beach huts in my homeless years. The smell of barbecues stirred up a hunger in my belly. I see friends and family in laughter. They were having a great time together. I sat on the sand. I wondered about life itself. I was not a part of the world. I made the sea my home. People were escaping the real world.

I did not care which world they were escaping. I was escaping from their reality. I noticed people laughing. Do they have that laughter in the real world, or do they just laugh beside the sea? It was God's plan for me not to have a beach hut. I know the reason why my life was not lived in the real world. Was God protecting me from the real world. The beach hut people were escaping from a stressful world. Jesus Christ said that we are not to be a part of the world.

Being homeless and unloved keeps you separated from the

world. I still do not have a beach hut. I realise that it cost so much. I am still as physically poor as I was when I was homeless. It has been years since I was homeless. I always return to the beach huts. I am now escaping the same world as the beach hut people. I always sit on the same bit of sand. I realise how lucky I was to have lived by the sea. I now get to escape the world with a pen and paper.

I can now write about how Jesus Christ dragged me away from the beach huts. I put Jesus Christ above the beach huts. Jesus Christ shelters me in the pouring rain. I do not need a beach hut for Jesus Christ to hear my cries. I am at home with the teachings of Jesus Christ. Jesus Christ said that I should not desire what others have. I can go to the beach on a winter's day. I can feel the power of the mighty sea. I sit here and I remember the young me. I am not homeless by the sea. Jesus Christ gave me a material home.

I am not hungry by the sea. Jesus Christ feeds me on his timeless words. I will hire a beach hut one day. I will sit there like the beach hut people. Anything is possible when you believe in Jesus Christ. I am different from the beach hut people. The beach hut people never spent their teenage years living by the sea. I lived and breathed the sea air. I always noticed the beach huts in the winter months. The beach huts were locked up in the night.

I could have slept in a colourful beach hut in the winter months. I would have been as snug as a bug in a rug. I had to lay my head on an old wooden bench. I looked to the moon and the stars. I would not of had the moon and stars if I had slept in a beach hut. That is the reason why Jesus Christ never gave me a beach hut in the winter. Was I richer than the people with beach huts? The beach hut people got to escape the world for a day. I got to escape the world for years when I was homeless by the sea. I do not desire to own a beach hut. I can sit on the sand and I know that Jesus Christ loves me.

70

Tearing a fishing net on the rocks

I am a fisher of men. I love to fish with a rod and line. I have Jesus Christ as my bait. I am also aware that there is a fishing net. I know that Satan has a net. I was caught in a net of drug addiction. The net of drug addiction dragged me around in a sea of guilt and shame. A lot of people are caught in Satan's net. Jesus Christ calls us to help the people who are caught in a net of despair. I know all about fishing nets. A fishing net gets dragged along the seabed.

A fishing net can be torn on the rocks. I want to snag the net of despair on the rocks. We could tear the net on the rocks. People would be set free from the net of despair. I believe that it can happen in my lifetime. We are all called to be a fisher of men. Not just men but the young and old. Some people think that they are free, so they sit back. They watch as the net drags people around in despair. The net of despair can easily scoop you up. I have seen it happening to people over the last ten years.

Life was good. People then found them self's struggling with depression. Their riches were lost in a financial crash. Their health had taken a turn for the worse. I have seen all sorts of people in the net of despair. People feel abandoned when they are caught in a net of despair. Jesus Christ rescued me from Satan's net of despair. I have been pulling sinners towards the cross. The net of despair cannot catch you when you are sitting at the foot of the cross.

Do you feel like you are caught in a net of despair? Jesus Christ wants you to rest in a net of amazing grace. We must pull the sinners from the net of despair. My drug infested council estate was caught in a net of despair. The people from my drug infested council estate suffered much in their lives. The net of despair is full of material stuff. People lust after material stuff, so they stay in the net of despair. Children are abused in the net of despair. The abused children grow up and they abuse drugs.

The net of despair is full of spiritual poverty. The Holy Bible tells us to separate ourselves from the net of despair. The Holy Bible does not tell us to forget about the people who are trapped in the net of despair. I want you to consider becoming a fisher of men. You could catch the lost souls who are perishing in a net of despair. The Holy Spirit has the power to tear the net of despair apart. I can only make a little tear in the net of despair. A few souls have escaped through that small tear.

Prayer has the power to split the net of despair apart. This is what happened in the revivals. Whole communities were set free from the net of despair. Thousands of people were set free at Pentecost. Jesus Christ came to make us fisher of men. I free people from the net of despair. I then cast my fishing rod towards them. Jesus Christ is my bait, so they take a bite. I hook them and Jesus Christ reels them into a net of amazing grace. Are you struggling to escape the net of despair? Jesus Christ can set you free if you believe.

71

Walking along a sandy beach with Jesus Christ

I was homeless. I used to walk along the sandy beach. I felt so free in my teenage years. I walked away from the concrete streets. My walking brought me to the waves of the sea. I was about a mile away from the concrete streets. I thought a lot as I walked on the sandy beach. I walked in the waves of the sea. The tide would start to turn on me. I would be pushed back to the concrete streets. The concrete streets were my home. I felt the sand below the waves of the sea.

My feet felt the little waves in the sand. The physical waves had made the waves in the sand. The tide started to push me back. I walked back to the concrete streets. I walked towards the drifting sand. The wind would blow the dry sand on to my wet feet. Its beauty can only be experienced when your homeless and unloved. The wind blew the sandy glass on to my wet feet. The drifting sand would then sting my dry feet.

One grain of sand is so small when it hits my feet. I realised that I was so small.

I felt small when I walked under a sunrise. I looked up to heaven. I prayed out to a God that I could not see. The invisible God placed a million stars in the sky above me. The incoming tide was racing in like a wild horse. I left footprints on the sandy beach. The tide started to wash my footprints under its waves. My footprints disappeared. I was left without a trace of life. Was I rich in my teenage years? I was free from walking on your concrete.

The concrete that builds your paths and roads will give you sore feet. It is a difficult life when you are walking on the concrete streets. You are free to lose your socks and trainers on a sandy beach. I am walking away with this short story. I just need to remember the wet sand. I found myself a small pool of water by the sea. I stood in the pool of water. I wiggled my toes. The incoming tide was about to push me back on to the concrete. I just wiggled my toes in a pool of water. My feet would slowly disappear into the wet sand.

I then found myself sitting on the concrete sea defence. I left my feet bare as I watched the tide covering the sand. The sun would dry my wet feet. I would rub the sand away from between my toes. I felt dirty when I was sleeping on the streets. I looked at my washed feet and I smiled. I always looked after my feet by the sea. My clothes stank. My feet where perfectly clean. I was born into a concrete world. My first steps where in a drug infested council estate.

I ran the streets in my teenage years. I left footprints in the sand. The waves washed my footprints away. I left bloody footprints on your concrete streets. Jesus Christ washed my bloody footprints away by his blood on the cross. You have left carbon footprints on this earth. Your footprints are stained in sin. Let Jesus Christ wash your footprints away in waves of his father's forgiveness. Look back on your life. You will see your carbon footprints. You can ask for forgiveness. Your sinful footprints will be washed clean when you walk towards the old, rugged cross.

72

Stuck below the waves of a spiritual sea

I look at the surface of the sea. I cannot see below its gentle waves. How deep does the sea go? How deep does my thoughts go? My thoughts can go deep. I was stuck below the waves of the sea. My drug addiction dragged me to the depths of despair. Do you feel like you are stuck below the waves of the sea? The depths of depression can sink you to the oceans floor. There are all sorts of weird creatures in the deep sea. I was like a creature in my teenage years.

I was stuck in the dark corners of the sea. Some creatures spend their whole lives at the bottom of the sea. The creatures have never seen the light of the sun. Could the creatures survive if they swam up to the surface of the sea. I found Jesus Christ and he lit up my life with his light. It was too bright for my hazy eyes. I swam away from the light of the world. A creature is commutable at the bottom of the sea. I was commutable living in the dark corners of the sea.

I started to swim towards the light of the world. My eyes adjusted to his amazing grace. Jesus Christ set me free from my drug addiction. My drug addiction had me hiding in the depths of the sea. I now see things with clear eyes. I also have a soft heart for the old, rugged cross. Are you scared to accept Jesus Christ as your light? Are you hiding in the depths of the sea? Come and swim up to the light of the world. Your eyes will adjust to his father's forgiveness.

So many people are hiding their dirty sins at the bottom of the sea. I was afraid to face the light of the world. I was hiding in the depths of the sea for years. I hid along the seafront for years. I was not a part of society in my teenage years. I thought that society could survive without me. I felt to dirty in my drug addiction. Jesus Christ opened my spiritual eyes. People in society where just as dirty as me. Their sins are hidden from people's eyes. Your deep sea could be your bedroom.

So many people isolate in their own homes. They are scared to face the world. I was the same in my teenage years. My deep sea was the sea front. I was isolating myself by the waves of the sea. Some people feel trapped in a concrete world. Jesus Christ is calling you out of your deep sea. You have become used to living in a deep sea. You do not have to hide your guilt and shame in the deep sea. I was forgiven at the cross. I have come out of my deep sea.

I am now dragging other people out of their deep sea. I have saved some people from isolation. I went to their homes and I brought them out into the light. I have done a lot over the last ten years. Bringing sinners out of their dark sea is the greatest thing that you can do. Some people spend their whole lives in isolation and depression. I will move mountains to drag someone out of their deep sea. Are you hiding in a deep sea of depression? Do not fear the lord Jesus Christ. My Jesus Christ is near to the people who fear. Jesus Christ brought me out of the deep sea and this short story is for you.

73

Stepping out of your boat to meet Jesus Christ

I felt safe in my boat when I was homeless. I found Jesus Christ and he asked me to step out of my boat. The disciples where in a fishing boat. Jesus Christ came alongside them. Jesus Christ beckoned his beloved disciple to edge of the fishing boat. Jesus Christ motioned for the disciple to step out of the fishing boat. The sea was stormy, and the disciples were afraid. The disciple steps on to the waves of the sea. The disciple starts to walk towards Jesus Christ.

The disciple looks to his left and he sees the waves of the stormy sea. The disciple took his eyes of Jesus Christ. The disciple starts to sink into the waves. Jesus Christ reached his hands out to the drowning disciple. Jesus Christ said oh you of little faith. Jesus Christ asked me to step out of my boat. I stepped out of my boat. I took my eyes of Jesus Christ. I started to sink into the waves of fear. Jesus Christ reached out to me in my hour of need. Would you step out of your boat to meet Jesus Christ on the waves of the sea.

Your boat is the things that stop you trusting in Jesus Christ. Is your boat full of worldly things? You may lose your boat of worldly things if you step out to meet Jesus Christ. I was lucky because my boat was full of bad things. I was homeless. I did not have worldly things. My boat was overloaded with guilt and shame. I stepped out of my boat ten years ago. I met Jesus Christ on the waves of the sea. I have been walking in amazing grace for the last ten years.

I had no problem stepping out of my boat in faith. I did jump back into my boat in the first few years. I kept on dipping in and out of my boat. It was hard to trust Jesus Christ. I was commutable in my boat of drug addiction. My old boat is no longer available to me. I stepped out of my boat. Jesus Christ led me into the real world. People in the real world are commutable in their boats. I was not commutable in the real world. I have kept walking in the real world. I have shown people how to step out of their boats.

Some people are afraid to trust in Jesus Christ. I know believers who have never taken that step. They are commutable working from their boats. Helping in a soup kitchen does not bring you out of your boat. Stepping out your boat on a Sunday does not bring you closer to Jesus Christ. I ended up diving out of my boat. Jesus Christ always met me on the waves of the sea. I have sunk into the waves a thousand times. Jesus Christ always reached his hands out to me.

What is stopping you from stepping out of your boat. Is Jesus Christ rocking your boat? Take a step of faith before your boat capsizes you into the waves. I know people who were commutable in their boats. Their boats were then capsized. These people found themselves drowning in a sea of pain. Jesus Christ was not there to pull them onto the waves. Trust in Jesus Christ today. You could find yourself drowning in the sea. We must step out of our boats in faith. Do not spend your life in a boat of selfishness. Step out your boat today. You will walk on the waves of amazing grace with Jesus Christ.

74

Picking a pebble up from a sandy beach

I love to walk along a pebble beach. The waves of the sea are rolling the pebbles around. The waves are shaping the pebbles. I love the crashing sound. I look at the pebbles on the beach. I spot one and I pick it up. The pebble is smooth to my eyes. Jesus Christ wanted to make me as smooth as my pebble. Why would Jesus Christ make me smooth? God intended us to be smooth from the beginning. Man wanted to be anything but smooth in God's eyes.

God sent Jesus Christ to dwell amongst us. Jesus Christ was to teach us how to become smooth in God's eyes. My smooth pebble is dirty looking. The dirtiness on my pebble was to resemble my sins. I spot a pure white pebble and I pick it up. I look to the sky. I remember my old life. I was a rough pebble in my teenage years. Jesus Christ rolled me around in waves of living waters. I started to become smooth in his father's eyes. I was a dirty pebble in my teenage years. Jesus Christ washed me clean in waves of living waters.

I started to become clean in his father's eyes. Therefore, I write my short stories. Are you a rough pebble in God's eyes? Jesus Christ can make you smooth in his father's eyes. Are you a dirty pebble in God's eyes? Jesus Christ can wash you clean in waves of living waters. I see people as pebbles in my short story. I know that I was a rough pebble. I know that my sinful life turned me into a dirty pebble. I am now smooth in my life. I am cleaner in my life. Jesus Christ is the greatest.

Jesus Christ loved me in my roughness. Jesus Christ loved me in my dirtiness. I found myself living in society. People appear to be smooth. People appear to be clean. I sat in my homelessness. I never denied that I was rough and dirty. My ugliness was visible to the eyes of society. My society is just kidding itself. Every human on the earth is imperfect. Jesus Christ was God's perfect pebble. Jesus Christ took my roughness on the cross. Jesus Christ took my dirtiness on the cross.

I want to be a perfect pebble in the eyes of God. Do your friends and family see you as a smooth pebble. Do your friends and family see you as a clean pebble. Stop fooling yourself and admit that you are imperfect. You cannot hide your roughness from God's eyes. You cannot hide your dirtiness from God's eyes. God wants you to become a perfect pebble. You will become smooth when you repent your sins. You will become whiter when you accept Jesus Christ into your heart.

I have taken a rough pebble to the cross. I see them becoming smooth. I have taken a dirty pebble to the cross. I see them becoming whiter. I just love the sea. I had to pick up a pebble to understand who Jesus Christ is. You are a pebble in the eyes of Jesus Christ. Will you let Jesus Christ turn you into a perfect pebble? I was not an attractive pebble when I was homeless. I am now a perfect pebble in the eyes of Jesus Christ. I pray that you will become a perfect pebble in the eyes of Jesus Christ.

75

A dog walker walking along a sandy beach

I slept on my bench in my homeless years. I would wake up to a sunrise. I was the first person to walk on the perfect beach. I would sit on my old bench after I walked on the beach. I started to see the dog walkers approaching the beach. I liked the dog walkers in my homeless years. A dog walker always said hello. Society ignored me by the beach and a dog walker would tell me a story. Why did a man need a dog to walk on the beach? I walked on the beach on my own.

Did the dog stop the man from feeling lonely? The gap in my soul could not be filled by having a dog. I talked with hundreds of dog walkers over the years. Man has tried everything to fill that lonely gap in his soul. I found the secret to feeling whole. The promise of the Holy Spirit filled me up. Some men have told me that they feel empty. They have a dog, and they are still searching for the missing piece. The missing piece is Jesus Christ. I thought that I was lonely by the sea.

The dog walkers had a family with a home. The dog walkers were searching for something on the sandy beach. They said hello to me. They then made their way onto the beach. I watched them as they looked out over the waves. I was always the first person to walk on the perfect beach. The dog walkers would arrive about seven o'clock in the morning. I was already walking on the beach at six o'clock. The dog walkers missed the sun coming up. I look back at the dog walkers.

The dog walkers were searching for something. I spent years by the sea. I was searching for something. I found Jesus Christ in my searching. I now have a dog and a home. My little dog is my best friend. Me and my dog have walked on this beach for years. I no longer search the sea like the dog walkers. I want to tell the dog walkers my own story. I noticed the loneliness in their eyes as they searched the sandy beach for answers. The answer is Jesus Christ. A fisherman will tell you a story.

A dog walker will tell you his life story. A dog walker never seemed to judge me in my homeless state. Society liked to remind you of your homeless state. Do you know a dog walker who goes to the beach? Do you know that he is searching the beach for answers to life? Give that dog walker a copy of my book. I am sure the beach will have more meaning to his life after he reads my short stories. I am going to print a hundred copies of this short story. I will walk along the beach.

I will hand them out to the men with dogs. I am just so happy that I found the answers to my life by the sea. I want to thank all the dog walkers who said hello to me. I was grateful that they never judged me in my homeless state. I little hello can brighten up a homeless person's morning. My mornings where spent walking on the beach in my homeless years. I am going to sit here for a little while. A dog walker may pass me today. I will share this story with him if he says hello to me. Jesus Christ is always working in my life. I am now a fisher of men.

76

Finding a sandy cove by the sea

I always wanted to find a sandy cove by the sea. A nice little cove with its own sandy beach would have done me. The tide would roll in at night. I would have been cut off from your world. I never found a sandy cove in my teenage years. I had to share the beach with drunken louts in a seaside resort. I always pictured my little cove. I wanted one with a rock face. I could have found a nice little cave in the rocks face. Heaven is like a sandy cove with a rock face.

Jesus Christ is like the cave in the rocks face. So many people are living on a sandy cove. The tide is rolling in with their fears. The tide cuts you of from the world. Imagine if you were trapped on a sandy cove. The incoming tide of fear has you trapped. You look at the rocks face and you spot a cave. You cannot climb the cliffs face because it is too steep. How would you feel if you felt that Jesus Christ was calling you into the cave? The cave face looks damp and dark.

The incoming tide is going to reach the entrance of the cave. You must decide what you are going to do. The tide of fear is lapping at your feet. Taking a step of faith is like stepping into the cave. My life was like that. I tried to climb the cliffs face. It was fruitless. I kept on fallen back down. I took a step into the cave. I made my way through the dark cave. I spotted a flickering light. I found Jesus Christ in a dark cave. I love the sea and Jesus Christ gave me this picture of a sandy cove.

Is Jesus Christ asking you to take a step of faith. People are stuck in a sandy cove. These people are cut off by the tide. They are stuck in isolation. I was living by the sea in my homelessness. I was cut off from the world. I watched the tide rolling in with my fears. I spotted a cave in the rocks face. Jesus Christ was drawing me into his light. Do not spend your life being cut off from Jesus Christ. I see a homeless person. I know that he is alone. The homeless person may as well be stuck in a sandy cove.

Society sees a homeless person as a waste of space. I know that Jesus Christ is calling him. The homeless person is scared to trust in Jesus Christ. The homeless person needs to take a step of faith. I was that homeless person. I took a step of faith. I entered the cave. My soul was cold and hungry. I walked towards the flickering light. My heart started to glow in the dark. I felt safe in the cave. The tide of fear could not reach me. My life was probably different to yours.

You will never know Jesus Christ unless you step into the cave. Your heart will always be cold if you do not find his light. I would get locked up in a mental hospital for writing this short story. I just pick up my pen and paper. A sandy cove popped into my head. This could be a story for a homeless person. Give a homeless person a copy of this short story. A homeless person is stuck on the streets. They maybe find a little shelter in my story. Imagine if they took a step of faith. Jesus Christ could change their lives with his light. We need to search for the light of the world in a dark cave.

77

Living on an island with Jesus Christ

I always wanted to live on an island by myself. I was homeless and isolated in my drug addiction. That is like being on an island. People never wanted to accept me on their island. I always lived my life on the verge of society. I lived by the sea, so I was on the verge of this island. You can run away from yourself. You will always run into the sea water. I was always on the run from the authorities. I also ran away from the people who wanted me dead. Some people can become isolated.

That is like being on an island. You cut yourself of from other people. I always put my back to this island. I looked out to the waves of the sea. We are living on an island because we are surrounded by the sea. I was surrounded by violence, so I escaped to the sea. I always wonder about one of the disciples. The disciple was put on to an island. The disciple freed himself from the world. The book of revelations was written by this disciple.

This disciple was able to connect with Jesus Christ in a personal way. I freed myself from being a slave to this island. I was able to hear Jesus Christ speaking to me. I have tried to show that through my short stories. Living on an island by myself would be peaceful. I used to watch the tide coming in. The sea water would surround a bit of sand. I would paddle through the sea water to get to that bit of sand. I would just sit there for a while. I enjoyed about half an hour's peace.

I watched the tide rising around me. My little island got smaller and smaller. The incoming tide can be dangerous. The tide can sneak around you. One minute you are walking on the sandy beach. The next thing you notice is that you are surrounded by sea water. I was never in danger when I sat on an island of sand. I knew the tides of the sea. Would you love to escape to a little tropical island by yourself? A lot of people could not survive the social isolation. I could survive the isolation on a tropical island.

I am still not a part of this island. I live and work in this island's concrete streets. I feel for the people who have never experienced the freedom that I had in my homeless years. Some people spent their lives in a concrete world. They are like robots in a funny sort of way. They desire what this island offers them. People become slaves to a materialistic world. Jesus Christ can set them free from that slavery. I spoke to a rich man a long time ago. I had just entered society for the first time in my life.

I had a job, and I was working forty hours a week. I was complaining about working my life away. This man told me that he had worked seven days a week for forty odd years. I nearly fell of my chair. This man was extraordinarily rich in material wealth. I told him about Jesus Christ. This man was not content in his life. I am always at the beach. I am always asking Jesus Christ to put me on an island by myself. This island is a selfish place to work and live. I will conform to working a forty-hour week, but I will never let it hold me a prisoner.

78
A harbour of safety for God's ships

I look at heaven as if it were a harbour. A harbour in heaven could keep God's ships safe. I did not have a harbour for the first thirty years of my life. There is not much shelter in a drug infested council estate. My family should have been a harbour of protection for me. What do kids do when they are born into a drug infested council estate. The children find their shelter in drug abuse. The drugs become an escape from the madness of life.

I never tried to find a harbour in my drug infested council estate. I sailed into the storms of violence. My drug infested council estate drew my blood from my flesh. I was beat up physical and emotionally. What about the children who never grew up in my drug infested council estate? They have been brought up in a working-class family or a middle-class family. They are then thrown into drug addiction. Ninety percent of drug addicts come from working-class families or middle-class families.

It is very damaging for them if they become homeless. I was lucky because my drug infested council estate is imprinted in my life. I had seen and suffered so much before I was even homeless. These working- or middle-class drug addicts could become mighty ships for God. I have tried to share Jesus Christ with the working- or middle-class drug addicts. They normally laugh or mock me in my faith. A drug addict from a drug infested council estate believes that God has a harbour for his ships.

I have shared Jesus Christ with a lot of drug addicts over the years. I just love to find one like me. I teach them about the harbour in heaven. They start to search for Jesus Christ. Would you love God to see you as a ship? We can enter a harbour of amazing grace when we believe in Jesus Christ. My short stories would have made sense to a different generation. I would love to have lived in the nineteen hundred or before. The sea was the highway of the world.

Everything was moved around by the sea. Harbours where part of everyone's life. Think of a time when the sea and ships where everything. The storms at sea where frighting. People knew the importance of harbours. Do you believe that heaven is like a spiritual harbour for our souls? Jesus Christ is the entrance to heavens harbour. A was caught in the spiritual storms all my young life. I was looking for a harbour for my battered soul. I found the entrance to heavens harbour.

Jesus Christ guided me into a harbour of amazing grace. The storms will not stop until Jesus Christ returns. A lot of ships will be turned away from God's harbour of amazing grace. Will you believe in my harbour of amazing grace? Do you feel like you are stuck in spiritual storms? Jesus Christ can calm your storms. Jesus Christ will then guide you into a harbour of amazing grace. Your broken soul will be mended. Jesus Christ will restore you into a mighty ship. I am a mighty ship for Jesus Christ. I am always pointing sinners towards a spiritual harbour of amazing grace.

79
Finding a calm sea in a stormy sea

A calm sea is something you wish for when you are stuck in a stormy sea. I knew that I was living in a stormy sea. I was drowning in my drug addiction. I was covering up a lot of guilt and shame. I am now in a calm sea with Jesus Christ. I can sail out my short stories from my calm sea. A calm sea with Jesus Christ can get choppy. I can live with a choppy sea today. I look at people in society. They are looking for a calm sea in their sinful life's.

I can understand the people who are born into a stormy sea. I struggle to understand the people who were brought up in a calm sea. Everyone will end up in a stormy sea. I was raised in the storms, so I weathered the storms. I grew up and I ended up in violent storms. I do not say mental as a word. Some people do not like to call themselves mental. I was mental in my teenage years. We can all suffer mental health storms in our life's. A storm of depression and anxiety is a mental health storm. I was left mentally damaged by my storms.

Jesus Christ guided me into a calm sea. My mind was made well. I am still a bit unstable at times but that is my life. Are you looking for a calm sea in your life? Is the sea raging against your sinful life. We should not be ashamed to admit that life is rough. There was a man who was going through a mental health storm. Jesus Christ crossed the sea of galilee to meet the man. The story is written in the Holy Bible. You can read the story on your own. Jesus Christ met this man just of the shoreline.

The man ran to Jesus Christ and he fell at his knees. Jesus Christ healed that man of his mental state. I look at the story of the man. I know that Jesus Christ has a healing touch. The man had been cutting himself with stones. We call that self-harming today. I know a lot of people who self-harm. It is an escape from the pressure that builds up inside. The storms of life will leave you feeling tense. Cutting yourself releases the fears and tears. I was self-harming in my teenage years.

I ran into the violent storms. My grief about losing my mother had to come out. I found peace from my grief when I met Jesus Christ on a sandy beach. My storms were greater than yours. My grief was not greater than anybody's. Losing a loved one will tip you over the edge. A loss can throw you into the storms. I want you to know that there is a calm sea. The disciples were caught in a storm at sea. They were physically terrified. Jesus Christ raised his hands over the physical sea.

The stormy sea settled like a baby in its mothers' womb. The disciples fear turned to joy. Jesus Christ can calm the physical sea and he can calm your emotional storms. Have a look at some of the disciples in the Holy Bible. Some of the disciples where unstable men. Jesus Christ never picked your average person to follow him. Jesus Christ was always around people who were not stable. I just want you to know that Jesus Christ is offering you a calm sea. I was caught in a stormy sea and Jesus Christ led me into a calm sea.

80
A luxury yacht and a raft of poverty

I am standing by a harbour today. I am looking at luxury yachts. I look back on my life today. I was not brought up in luxury. I grew up on a raft of poverty. I lived like a hunted animal in my teenage years. I was living on a raft of poverty. Other people were living in luxury yachts. I sat homeless in my raft of poverty. People sailed by me in their luxury yachts. I sat begging on the streets. There dirty looks reminded me that I was living on a raft of poverty.

I knew that I was living in a physical raft of poverty. My soul was also living on a raft of spiritual poverty. That spiritual poverty was not visible to the eyes of society. My society judged my outward appearance. Jesus Christ looked at my inward appearance. Jesus Christ touched my soul with his father's forgiveness. My soul was transformed into a luxury yacht. I really felt like I was sailing in luxury. Does your soul feel like it is sailing in a raft of spiritual poverty? Your outward appearance could resemble a luxury yacht.

Jesus Christ knows that your soul is sailing in a raft of spiritual poverty. A homeless person knows that he is sailing in a raft of physical poverty. I was the same in my teenage years. The homeless persons soul is also sailing on a raft of spiritual poverty. I want the world to know about my luxury yacht. It is not visible to your sinful eyes. My soul is sailing in a luxury yacht. I was confused when my life was turned upside down.

Why would Jesus Christ care if my soul were sailing in a raft of spiritual poverty. Jesus Christ cared because I believed in his name. I honestly believe in the promises of Jesus Christ. I absolutely love Jesus Christ with all my heart and soul. I love Jesus Christ for given me the wisdom to write a book of short stories. I learned about the sea because I lived by the sea. How does Jesus Christ see you in your life? Does Jesus Christ see you sailing in a luxury yacht? Or does he see you sailing in a raft of spiritual poverty. I got to know people in society.

They were sailing in a luxury yacht. They always look down at the homeless beggars. They criticise them for being a waste of space. Its visible to see that a homeless person is living on a raft of physical poverty. We should not judge the people who are living on rafts of physical poverty. We are left spiritually poor when we judge the people who are living on rafts of physical poverty. How would you describe your soul to your friends and family?

Your friends and family can see that you are sailing in a

luxury yacht of material wealth. You know how poor your soul is. Would you love to experience the love of Jesus Christ in your heart? Would you love to sail through your life in a yacht of spiritual riches? The spiritual riches go unseen by blind eyes. Try and not judged a homeless person on the streets. The homeless person knows that he is living on a raft of physical poverty. I lived on a raft of physical poverty. I am now writing my short stories from a luxury yacht. My soul became rich when I invited Jesus Christ into my life.

81
Watching the tides of the sea

I watched the tides rolling in and out for years. What power did God give to the moon? The moon has the power to draw the sea back and forth. The tides are to stop the sea from becoming stagnant. The tides give life to the creatures below the sea. I wonder about the land that man has claimed from the sea. Is the tide starting to claim its land back? Can man push his sins back and forth like the tide of the sea? I wonder if we could push the darkness out of this sinful island. I found Jesus Christ.

I can now push the darkness out of my life. The darkness will roll in like the tide. I am not a pushy person, but I must push the darkness away. It is like a game in my life. Darkness pushes itself in and I push it back out with prayer. Some people are not prepared to pray to Jesus Christ. A tide of darkness has washed itself into their lives. They cannot push it back with prayer. I have a plan and it is to warn people about a tide of darkness.

Do you feel like a tide of darkness has rolled over your life? It is time to push it back with Jesus Christ. I have Jesus Christ on my side. I know people and they accept that a tide of darkness has claimed their lives. I have the power of the moon at my fingertips. The moon can pull the tide away from a sandy beach. I can pull a tide of darkness away from a person's life. I can roar out with my prayers. I have watched this world over the last ten years.

People where blind to the tide of darkness. The tide of darkness has washed itself over this sinful land. The tide of darkness does not affect me when I am sitting at the sea. The world behind me is being washed in a tide of darkness. The tide of darkness is full of loneliness. People are cut off from knowing Jesus Christ. The tide of darkness is causing a wave of mental health. People are cut off from a healing touch from Jesus Christ. I am looking for an army of people who are prepared to pray.

We could push the tide of darkness away from our innocent children. We could put a sea defence around their innocent souls. We can only do that by praying for the power of the moon. A tide of darkness was washing itself over the streets of Jerusalem. The Holy Spirit fell at Pentecost. The disciples burst into the streets. The tide of darkness was pushed back. The lame was healed and minds where restored. The disciples travelled far and wide.

The disciples entered villages and people seen the light of Jesus Christ. The villages became sanctuaries for the broken. Revivals have broken out over the centuries. Whole communities were set free from the tide of darkness. Do you believe that we can push the tide of darkness out of this land? I will stand by this sea. I will pray for a revival. I have helped individual people over the years. I watched them pushing the darkness out of their lives. I then seen Jesus Christ pushing a light into their lives. I am just a humble man who was once a broken teenager. I am now living in the light of Jesus Christ.

82

The end of my book

I thank you for reading my book of short stories. I have been on a journey of discovery. I have changed so much over the last ten years. I wonder if my short stories have you considering what life is about. Life was a mystery to me in my teenage years. I am now a grown man. My life does have a meaning. The Holy Bible is not just a book of stories. The Holy Bible is a living book. Jesus Christ transformed my life. My young life was shaped by the sea.

This world is a crazy place to live. You can seek Jesus Christ in your life. I hope my short stories have shown you my love for Jesus Christ. I pray that you will look at the young homeless people in a different light. My heart bleeds for the homeless people. I grew up in a criminal world. My family was well known in a criminal world. I was street wise before I could even walk. A lot of young homeless are not street wise. Please give a homeless person a copy of this book. This book could change a homeless person's life.

Printed in Great Britain
by Amazon

63093593R00108